GRIT
&
GRACE

GRIT
&
GRACE

RESTORING THE FEMININE SOUL

MELODY BROCK LOVVORN

Grit & Grace: Restoring the Feminine Soul

Copyright © 2026 by Melody Brock Lovvorn

Soul Care Press
Birmingham, Alabama 35242
melodylovvorn.com

Library of Congress Control Number: 2026904857

ISBN (hardcover): 979-8-9948742-0-2
ISBN (paperback): 979-8-9948742-1-9
ISBN (ebook): 979-8-9948742-2-6

Names, identifying details, and certain circumstances have been changed to protect the anonymity of individuals portrayed in the illustrations herein.

This book is intended for informational and spiritual encouragement purposes only and is not a substitute for professional counseling, medical care, or mental health treatment. If you are in danger or need immediate help, please contact local emergency services.

Cover design: Soul Care Press
Interior illustrations: rylocreative.com (@RyloCreative)
Editor: Stacy K.

First edition
Printed in the United States of America

For Ryland, Tal, Gabe, Hannah,
Hudson, Keller, and Lively Grace—
with all my love

CONTENTS

Foreword _______________________________________13

Prologue: The Holy Tension of a Woman's Heart ______17

Author's Note _________________________________27

Part I. Radiance by Design

Before the fracture, we remember the original.

1. The Girl God Placed in You _________________31

Before the noise. Before the pain. Before the expectations.

2. The Divine Order We Were Meant For ________45

Identity before intimacy. Belonging before relationship. Worth before work.

Part II. Fracture and Survival

How radiance dims, then breaks — without shame.

3. When Radiance Began to Fracture ___________63

How life begins to teach a girl to disappear.

4. Where Radiance Breaks____________________81

Some breaks don't shatter you; they reveal the woman you were always meant to become.

5. Forgetting Her Radiance___________________93

What the soul learns when love feels uncertain.

Part III. Receiving What Was Missing

Care, presence, protection—and the love that stays.

6. The Mother Wound: Will I be cared for? _______________ 105
Where our need for care was formed—and where God meets it.

7. The Father Wound: Will I be Protected? _______________ 125
Where our need for protection and blessing was formed—and where God meets it.

8. Letting God Re-Parent the Soul _______________ 137
Receiving what was missing.

Part IV. Identity Restored

Now identity can be received, not performed.

9. The Rib: Her Blueprint of Identity _______________ 149
The sacred architecture of feminine belonging.

10. Sacred Ground: Meeting Yourself Honestly_______________ 167
When the counseling room becomes holy ground.

Part V. Becoming Whole

Healing moves from insight to embodiment.

11. The Four Gifts of the Feminine Soul _______________ 187
Remembering what was always there.

12. Motherhood Through Restoration_______________ 215
When healing reshapes generations that come after you.

13. Becoming Whole: Reuniting the Protector and the Rib_241
Where grit and grace become partners.

Part VI. The Threshold

The invitation to sit.

14. Making Room for the Girl Inside _______________________269

Regulation. Safety. Receiving.

15. Radiance Restored_____________________________________281

From healing to inheritance.

Epilogue: A Blessing for the Feminine Soul___________289

Faith that can breathe.

FOREWORD

Most of us step into life carrying hopeful expectations.
We imagine a future that will unfold with beauty and meaning.
Relationships that will feel safe and steady.

Dreams that will grow into something lasting.

We expect that if we love well, work hard, and walk faithfully,
life will slowly become what we once imagined.

But life rarely unfolds exactly the way we hoped.

Sometimes the path leads through valleys we never expected—
places where dreams shift, relationships change, and the quiet
beliefs we held about ourselves, about others, and even about
God begin to fracture.

In those moments, many women find themselves asking deeper
questions:

Who am I now?
What is still true?
And where is God in the middle of this story?

It is into these sacred and often tender questions that *Grit &*
Grace gently speaks.

This is not simply a book about relationships or life circumstances.
It is a journey back to identity—back to the place where a woman
remembers who she is, whose she is, and how grace slowly restores
what disappointment, devastation, and loss once tried to redefine
in her story.

Melody's story is one expression of the journey many women
know.

She entered adulthood carrying a deep belief in the goodness of love, faith, and commitment, shaped by the example of devotion and perseverance she witnessed in our home. She approached the blessing of marriage with hopeful expectations, believing it would be a place of shared love, faithfulness, and the wonder of building a life together.

But life does not always unfold according to the hopes we carry.

There were seasons when the path before her became far more difficult than she had imagined, seasons that tested her heart, her identity, and her faith in ways few people anticipate when they first step into love and commitment.

I watched my daughter walk through valleys no parent wishes for their child, yet I also witnessed the quiet strength and grace God formed within her through those very places.

Over the course of thirty years serving as a hospital chaplain and leading the hospital's chaplaincy team, I had the privilege of sitting beside people during some of the most sacred and difficult moments of their lives. Hospital rooms have a way of stripping away the illusions we often carry. In those quiet spaces, when the machines hum softly and the world outside seems to pause, people begin asking the deepest questions of the human heart.

I have listened as patients spoke honestly about their regrets, their fears, their broken relationships, and the longing to know that their lives still held meaning. I have seen strong individuals brought to tears as they wrestled with disappointment, loss, and the fragile nature of hope.

Again and again, I saw that even in the midst of pain, the human heart still longs for grace—to know that broken places can be restored and that the story of our lives is not finished. As both a chaplain and a father, those moments taught me that human hearts are far more fragile than we often admit, yet also far more resilient than we imagine.

The pages that follow are not written from a place of theory or easy answers. They emerge from Melody's own journey through suffering and healing—a journey that required tremendous grit and through which the grace of God slowly began to restore what life had wounded.

Melody writes with the same compassion and attentiveness that has marked her work with women for many years, creating space for readers to slow down, breathe, and remember that their own stories matter.

As I have watched Melody walk with many women through seasons of deep pain and transition, it has become clear to me that the compassion and wisdom reflected in these pages are not simply learned, but formed through both her own journey and her faithful care for others.

In my years walking beside people through crisis, I often witnessed how the valleys of life become the places where the deepest growth occurs.

If your own journey has included disappointment, loss, betrayal, or questions you never expected to ask, you may find something familiar within these pages. And if all you know is that you are weary, a little lost, or no longer feel like yourself, these words may feel like a companion on the way.

My hope is that as you read,
you will discover what Melody herself discovered . . .
that even in the valleys we never planned to walk,
grace has a way of meeting us, restoring us,
and gently reminding us who we truly are.

William Patrick Brock, Th.M., M.R.E.
Retired Hospital Chaplain
Past President, College of Chaplains
Father of the Author

PROLOGUE:
THE HOLY TENSION
OF A WOMAN'S HEART

I didn't realize how long I had been holding my breath until I walked into the hospital room to meet my granddaughter.

The light was soft,
almost holy,
resting over my daughter as she cradled her newborn.

Her hands moved with instinct and tenderness—
the same tenderness I once practiced with her when she was small.

When I held that tiny body against my chest,
something in me loosened.
Not dramatically.
But quietly.
Like a breath finally released after years of being held without notice.

In that moment, I remembered something sacred:

there is a part of a woman's heart that was designed—
and always meant—
for gentleness.
For beauty.
For nurture.
For presence.

And when I say *woman*, I mean you, the one reading this.

Your heart.
Your story.
Your body.
Your becoming.

If you've opened these pages and felt something stir—
a longing,
an ache,
a familiarity you can't quite name—
I want you to know this right away:

You are safe here.

We will move slowly—
at the pace your breath can follow—
until the girl inside you feels seen and held.

And I want to name you, specifically,
because women disappear inside generalities.

If you are a young girl, still forming, still tender, still learning what love sounds like—there is **nothing wrong** with your softness.

If you are a college girl, bright and stretching into the world, trying to find your place—your desire for love and belonging is **not weakness**. It is a holy longing.

If you are a young woman out of college, watching friends get engaged, wondering if you've missed your moment, praying for a husband and also trying not to ache—this book will **not shame** your desire. It will steady you in who you are while you wait.

If you are a new mother, overwhelmed by love and exhaustion, learning to carry life while you are still trying to find your own footing—you are **not failing**. You are becoming.

If you are a divorced woman, or a woman whose story did not turn out the way she hoped—your life is not over. God is not done. And your heart is **not disqualified**.

If you are an empty nester, living in the tender ache of letting go, asking, *Who am I now?*—you are **not forgotten** in this season. There is still calling here. There is still beauty.

If you are a grandmother, watching legacy bloom and carrying both joy and grief at once—this book will **honor** the holy weight you carry.

And **if you are a woman who cannot even name her season** because everything feels blurred—if you're simply trying to find your way back to yourself—then **you are exactly who I wrote for**, too.

In this book, **grit** is the strength you used to endure— and **grace** is the love that meets you underneath it.

And healing often looks like learning how to hold both.

A Breath Released

Watching my daughter become a mother stirred memories of the girl I once was.

Long before life asked me to be careful.
Long before I learned how to contain myself.

I grew up on the water, wild and full of wonder,
the salt air tangling my hair as my sisters and I raced barefoot
across the dock.

The world felt wide then.
Safe.

Running, I was always running—
across the grass,
or down by the water,
trying to find where my father was.

But I didn't know it then.

Sunlight danced on the waves,
laughter carried on the breeze,
and my father's presence,
steady in the background,
had been with me all along.

Inside our home,
my mother moved with quiet grace—
cooking,
nurturing,
creating warmth with her hands
in ways only mothers seem to know how to do.

My childhood held both structure and freedom,
like a shoreline meeting the sea.

I moved through it bright-eyed and unfiltered,
fully myself—
before the world ever suggested *I should be less.*

But slowly,
subtly,
I learned to soften my edges.

Not because anyone told me to.
Not because I was scolded or shamed.

But because I learned,
the way children do, to read the room.

In church, girls were praised for being sweet and still.
In school, good behavior mattered more than curiosity.
In sports, discipline outweighed delight.
In families, emotions were managed rather than explored.

No one asked me to shrink.
But I felt the invisible lines.
What made adults smile.
What made them uncomfortable.
What earned approval.
What disrupted peace.

And like so many girls,
I learned to adjust before I ever learned to listen to my own heart.

I became agreeable.

Responsible.
Capable.

Contained.

Not because anyone demanded it—
but because belonging quietly required it.

This is where the earliest shifts begin.
Not in trauma we can point to easily,
but in the subtle places where a girl begins trading pieces of her
radiance for acceptance.

If that sounds familiar—
if something in your body recognizes that exchange—
pause here.

Nothing is wrong with you.

This is where grit begins—how you learned to endure.
And this is where grace will meet you—where you begin to
come home.

This book will not ask you to untangle everything at once.
We are simply noticing where the forgetting began.

In my story, the forgetting began quietly—
long before anything dramatic happened.

Those early messages didn't announce themselves.
They settled in like background music—
always playing,
always shaping.

Be soft . . . but not too soft.
Be strong . . . but not too strong.
Be helpful.
Be pleasant.
Be small.

And so the arc of my life unfolded.
I married right after college,
believing godliness and effort would be enough to hold a
marriage steady.

I became a mother,
and something holy split open in me—
tenderness and fierceness intertwined.

And then, at thirty-one,
the life I had worked so hard to hold together began to crack.

Not suddenly.
But with the quiet, devastating force of truth rising to the surface.

Betrayal has a way of doing that.
It unravels everything we thought was stable.
It exposes the cost of all the ways we learned to adapt.

And yet—even in the breaking—
something deeper was stirring.
Not destruction.
But remembering.

There was one place I never learned to shrink:

with God.

I met Him early,
at the age of eight,
still wild,
still barefoot,
still running under open sky and water wide enough to breathe
in fully.

I never felt like *too much* with Him.

He was the place I felt seen without being measured.

I know that is not every woman's story.
Many women learned to perform even for God.

But hear me:

even if faith has felt complicated,
even if church has not always felt safe,
the God who made you is not asking you to become less.

And I did not yet understand the radiance He had woven into
me.
I did not know that the parts of myself I kept tucking away
were the very parts He meant to restore.

And so life taught me strength.

The quiet kind.
The necessary kind.

The kind you learn when falling apart is not an option.

When children need breakfast,
stability,
and bedtime prayers . . .
When someone has to hold the center—
and that someone is you.

This is the strength women rarely talk about.
Some women learn it early.

Some much later.

Strength born not from confidence,
but from necessity.
Forged in unseen places.

Worn like armor no one ever meant to own.
And yet—
beneath all of that strength,
something refused to die.

A softness beneath the armor.
A shimmer beneath the strain.
A radiance God had woven on purpose.

Life tried to bury it.

But it did not erase it.

It only hid it.

And what hides can be found.

What fractures can be restored.
What dims can be rekindled.

Radiance does not disappear.
It waits.

This book is not here to ask you to admire my becoming.
It is here to sit with you as you listen to your own.

Because when God restores a woman,
He rarely keeps it contained.

Restoration spills.

It becomes shelter.

It becomes legacy.

So here is my invitation:

Take a deep breath.
Set down the armor—just for a moment—
the armor you wore because protection didn't always come easily.

I will walk beside you as you remember who you were
before life required you to be strong.
And the woman you are still becoming—
because He is not finished.

You were made from the rib—
close to the heart,
near the breath—
formed to guard what is sacred
and carry what is holy.

You were made for connection.
You were made to breathe life.
You were made to heal, to tend, to shine.

In every season of womanhood,
and every season of motherhood.

And the God who authored your beginning
is not done writing your restoration.
Not even close.

We will begin at the very beginning—
where God first whispered who you are.
Before we talk about what happened to you,
we begin with what God placed in you.

AUTHOR'S NOTE

I am so honored that you are here.

This book was inspired by the birth of my first grandchild,
but it was born from deeper places too—
from my own story and from years of walking with women
through many seasons of life:

joy and loss, transition and longing, faith and questions. It also
grew from a deep desire to help women feel seen, held, and
gently led back to the heart of God.

My children—Ryland, Tal, Gabe, and Keller—are among my
greatest treasures on this earth, and Hudson and Hannah have
become beloved parts of the family we hold so dearly. The lives and
families they are building continue to remind me that restoration
and grace unfold across generations.

Wherever you are in your story, you belong here.

I have written this book slowly on purpose.

Many of the women who will find these pages are already carrying
more than their bodies were meant to hold.

So I wanted each word to have room to breathe. You are not
meant to rush through this work. Let it meet you at the pace of
your soul.

Throughout these pages, I sometimes imagine what biblical
characters may have felt or experienced in moments Scripture
does not describe in detail. I also sometimes apply verses to Eve

that were originally spoken to Israel or to the Church. I do this not to add to Scripture, but because I believe the whole Bible reveals the heart of the same God.

The God who delighted in Israel is the God who formed Eve.
The breath that raised dry bones is the breath that first filled human lungs.
The love David celebrated in the Psalms is the love that named Eve before Adam could.

Where I imagine—
I am offering reverent reflection, not historical certainty.
Where I apply Scripture analogically—
I am trusting that God's character is consistent, and that what He reveals of Himself in one place can help illuminate what He was doing in another.

My hope is that this approach honors the authority of Scripture while also helping you meet the living God within its pages.

Scripture is woven throughout these chapters not as something to master, but as an invitation to remember who God says you are.

Move gently.
Pause often.
Let grace lead the pace.

PART I

RADIANCE BY DESIGN

Before the fracture, we remember the original.

Chapter 1

THE GIRL GOD PLACED IN YOU

Before the noise. Before the pain.
Before the expectations.

> "Arise, shine, for your light has come."
> —Isaiah 60:1

In the heart of every girl,
there is a sacred spark,
a flicker of wonder,
a whisper of identity,
a longing planted by the God who dreamed her into being.

Before we ever learned to behave,
before we learned to compare,
before we learned to shrink or strive or apologize for existing,
we were little girls who moved with unfiltered joy.

Girls who believed beauty was holy.
Girls who trusted their desires.
Girls who lived with open hands, open hearts, open wonder.

Even if you've forgotten her,
your body remembers,
your imagination remembers,
your soul remembers the girl you once were—
because before the world shaped you,
God shaped you.

This chapter is about remembering what was true before anything
tried to rename you.

Before we played with dollhouses and wrapped dolls in blankets,
before we played dress-up and twirled with abandon,
before we learned to tuck our emotions into the corners of our chest,
we were responding to something ancient and divine within us.

The pull toward beauty,
the desire to nurture,
the longing to create,
connect,
protect,
and belong were not socialized into us;
they were written into us from Eden.

The world did not give us our tenderness or our imagination.
It did not give us our laughter or our fierce loyalty.
It did not give us our longing to be known,
chosen,
delighted in,
or safe.

Those were placed in us by God Himself.

Before the distortion.
Before the disappointment.
Before the fracture.

There is a girl inside us still—
a girl radiant by design—
waiting to be remembered.

The Longing Before the Dollhouse

Before we ever picked up a doll
or tied a blanket around our shoulders like a cape,
something was already stirring inside us—
a longing older than childhood,
older than memory,
older than the world itself.

It is the ache every woman knows
but struggles to name.

The ache that lived in us before language
and long before the world told us who we *should be*.

Many women carry three God-shaped longings woven into us by design[1]:

**the desire to be the beloved,
the longing to play a life-giving role in a story bigger than herself,
and the yearning to be at the center of a faithful, committed
love story.**

These desires were alive in us
long before we pretended to be princesses,
or moms,
or explorers,
or teachers.

The longing to be seen—
to be chosen,
delighted in,
pursued—
not for our performance,
but for our presence . . .

Because the feminine soul
was made to be a beloved daughter of God—
held in His gaze,
named with tenderness,
and kept without shame.

The longing to matter—
to be needed,
to be invited,
to step into a story bigger than ourselves . . .

This longing was planted in you
before you ever knew what romance was.

Because love is not meant to be watched from the outside.

We were designed to be woven into purpose—
to belong to something holy
and to be entrusted with meaning.

The longing to be at the center of a faithful,
committed love story—
a love that is steady,
a love that does not leave when we are vulnerable,
a love that holds our heart without requiring us to shrink . . .
a love that makes room for who we are becoming.

A love that says, again and again:

You are safe with me.

These longings are not flaws.

They are not fantasies.
They are not fragile or foolish.

They are **Edenic echoes—**
divine desires God planted in Eve
before the world fractured.

They are the pulse beneath our girlhood games,
the current beneath our imagination,
the spark in our eyes when we dressed up,
gathered treasures,
or created whole worlds from nothing.

Before we ever created imaginary worlds,
we were already responding to the divine one.

Before we ever played pretend,
we were practicing truths our souls already knew.

Before the messages that taught us
to be small, quiet, pleasing, or good,
there were holy desires alive in us—
desires the world would later call too much,
even when God called them good.

Creation Speaks the Same Language

Creation has always spoken the same language as the feminine soul.

The forest path that feels like a sanctuary.
The ocean that makes your lungs open without asking.
The stillness of a mountain peak that silences the inner noise you
didn't know you were carrying.
The way a rainbow after a storm makes even the most exhausted
woman stop and lift her eyes.

Whether she is a hiker or a homebody,
whether she loves wide skies or warm porches,

whether she feels most herself in deep woods or candlelit
rooms—
nature awakens the same ancient ache:

the longing to return to something true,
to something whole,
to something we were made for.

> "He has also put eternity in the human heart."
> —Ecclesiastes 3:11

Creation remembers Eden—
and so does the feminine soul.

Why Stories Speak to Our Souls

Stories reach us because they speak the same language God used
when He formed us.

We feel something awaken when we walk through the wardrobe
into *Narnia*, because our hearts were made for worlds where
courage and goodness win—
worlds that remind us of the garden we lost and the kingdom we
long for.

We follow the heroes of *Braveheart*
because we were designed to live inside a cosmic battle
between darkness and light,
between fear and courage,
between captivity and freedom.

We melt into the longing of *Pride and Prejudice*
because we were crafted for connection, truth, pursuit, and
chosen-ness—
the very things God breathed into His daughters from the beginning.

We cry during *Little Women*
because sisterhood speaks the language of our feminine design.
It echoes the first woman's radiance—
warmth shared, beauty multiplied, hearts woven together.

We cheer for Elsa and Anna in *Frozen*
because deep inside, we know:

love is supposed to heal, not wound.
Sacrifice is supposed to restore, not destroy.
Sisters—whether by blood or by heart—were meant to bring
one another home.

We dance with Donna and Sophie in *Mamma Mia!*
because something in their story feels like our own—
the questions of where we come from,
the ache of what was hidden,
and the hope that a woman's story doesn't end at motherhood.

We remember that joy is not frivolous—
it's healing,
and that sometimes the bravest thing a woman does is choose
herself again—
surrounded by the women who loved her before she remembered
how to love her own life.

The past doesn't have to be a prison;
it can become the music that carries you back to yourself.

These stories don't create longing.
They **awaken** it.
They stir the memory of Eden still humming in our bones.
They call out the radiance placed in us long before the world
taught us to dim it.

Salt, Sun, and Sisterhood

I remember growing up on the water—
sun on my shoulders, salt on my skin,
wet towels draped across the dock,
bare feet slapping against wood as my sisters and I ran wild and
free.

We were each other's first tribe—
three girls woven together before we knew what sisterhood
meant.

I was a twin, six minutes older,
with an older sister just twenty-two months ahead of us.

We were loud, imaginative, tender, dramatic, inseparable—
a storm and a symphony all at once.
And inside that little world we created,
our imaginations reigned without question.

We built entire cities from dollhouses.
We lined up stuffed animals like students waiting for very
important life lessons.
We wrapped baby dolls in blankets
with the seriousness of nurses guarding newborn hearts.
We played house, school, hospital, store—
never realizing we were rehearsing something holy.

We were practicing belonging.
We were practicing beauty.
We were practicing the kind of nurture and creativity
God had stitched into our design long before we named it play.

What looked like pretend
was actually the beginning of purpose.

But not every girl lived only in the world of dolls.

Some of us lived in two worlds—
and I was one of them.

We could rock a baby doll with tenderness one minute,
then sprint barefoot toward the woods as if the earth itself had
called our name.

We climbed trees, scraped our knees,
raced our bikes to the edge of the neighborhood,
and dove into the water with the kind of wild freedom
that made us feel alive in a way nothing else did.

Some girls felt closest to God while tucking a doll into a blanket.
Some felt Him in the quiet corners of their imagination.
And some of us felt Him in the wind tangling our hair,
in the mud between our toes,
in the deep breath you take right before you leap off the dock.

Both worlds are expressions of feminine radiance.
Both are reflections of the girl God placed inside us.
Both are valid, holy, beautiful beginnings.

Because long before a woman ever learns the theological language
for it, she instinctively knows how to:

create beauty,
cultivate connection,
protect what matters,
tend to the hurting,
and carry life wherever she goes.

Girls don't have to be taught this.
They *just do it.*

We thought we were pretending.
But we were practicing Eden.

Girls don't learn radiance—
they remember it.

Every game, every dream,
every wild adventure was our soul practicing Eden.

The Theology We Practiced Before Words

If you watch little girls long enough—
across cultures, generations, temperaments, and timelines—
you will see the same holy patterns unfolding:

Beautifying rooms without being asked.
Comforting the hurting with a seriousness far beyond their age.
Creating belonging out of almost nothing—
a blanket fort, a clubhouse, a circle of stuffed animals where
everyone has a place.

Holding imaginary babies as if they already understand reverence.
Offering kindness without instruction.
Building tiny worlds where no one is left out.

These aren't just childhood behaviors.
They are the earliest expressions of feminine theology—
the way we image God through nurture, beauty, and belonging.

We were practicing,
long before we knew it,
the very way God designed us to move through the world—
as nurturers,
as protectors,
as women who hold space—
to bring life,
to make a home,
both physical and emotional,
simply by being who we are.

And we did it with:

effortless joy,
unselfconscious freedom,
a radiance we hadn't yet learned to hide.

All of this existed *before* the world handed us its messages
about who we were supposed to be.

Before the noise.
Before shame crept in.
Before comparison whispered.
Before the pressure to perform.
Before the fallenness of others touched our sense of self.

We were radiant.

Not because we earned it.
But because *we were designed that way.*

> "God saw all that He had made,
> and it was very good indeed."
> —Genesis 1:31

But as we grew, something shifted.

The voices around us grew louder
than the voice within us.

The world began telling us who to be,
what to suppress,
what to strive for,
what to hide.

And slowly—so slowly we didn't notice—
the radiance we carried so naturally
began to dim.

Because no girl loses her radiance all at once.
It is never a sudden collapse.

It is erosion.
A thousand tiny messages, spoken and unspoken,
that teach her to forget who God made her to be.

Somewhere in your story,
those messages began to gather.

Maybe it was a classroom.
A living room.
A church hallway.
A locker room.
A dinner table.
A relationship that taught you to quiet your voice
or guard your softness
or shrink your joy.

Maybe it was a sharp word,
a quiet dismissal,
a look that told you
you were too much
or not enough
or somehow both at once.

But before all of that—
before the dimming,
before the pleasing,
before the adjusting—
there was a girl
who lived wide open.

A girl who built worlds from blankets and belief.
A girl who choreographed living room dances
like her body remembered Eden.
A girl who climbed trees, dove into oceans,
or wrapped baby dolls with fierce tenderness
because she instinctively knew
how to hold what was precious.

So before we go any further,
before we talk about the dimming or the fractures or the breaking,

I want you to pause here:

Let yourself remember her.

Where do you see her shining most freely?
What did her radiance look like
before the world told her to tone it down?

And when do you first remember
that light beginning to dim?

Let this remembering be gentle.
There is no shame here.
Only a return.

Because the girl God placed inside you
is not lost.

She is waiting.

And this—
this book, this journey, this remembering—
is how we begin to bring her home.

Chapter 2

THE DIVINE ORDER
WE WERE MEANT FOR

*Identity before intimacy. Belonging before
relationship. Worth before work.*

Because the girl God placed in you wasn't only radiant—
she was rooted.

Her radiance had a home:

the love-order of Eden.

And when that order is disrupted,
a woman doesn't just hurt . . .
she loses her center.

> "I praise You,
> because I have been remarkably and
> wondrously made."
> —Psalm 139:14

Before we learned to perform
or apologize or disappear,
God wrote a rhythm into creation—
an inner sequence that makes the human heart whole.

It is simple:

God → Yourself → Others

That's the only order in which identity stays intact.

We see this order first in Adam,
but we feel this order most deeply in Eve—
the first woman to ever breathe in God's world
without fear, comparison, or confusion.

Eve's First Relationship: God

When Eve opened her eyes for the very first time,
the gaze that met her wasn't Adam's.

We cannot know exactly what she saw in that first conscious
moment—
Scripture doesn't give us those details.
But what we can know is this:

before Eve ever looked into another human face,
she was already fully known by the God who had just formed her.

Adam was still sleeping when God completed this sacred work.
And though the text doesn't describe Eve's first experience,
it invites us to imagine something profound:

Scripture slows down to show us that moment,
as if heaven itself is whispering:

Before anyone else names you . . . you are Mine.

And so her first gaze was God —
the One who had already named her.

> "Do not fear, for I have redeemed you;
> I have called you by name; you are mine."
> —Isaiah 43:1

Before Eve ever stepped into a role,
before she became partner, helper, beauty, or strength,
she lived for one quiet breath in a world
where only she and God existed.

Her first inhale was oxygen.
Her first exhale was worship.

Her first awareness was being seen by the One who crafted her.

Not generally.
Not casually.
Not as one creation among many,
but intimately, intentionally,
with divine affection.

Imagine it:

Eve awakening in a garden crafted by the same hands that shaped
her. Light filtering through leaves not yet touched by decay.

Her lungs filling—
literally, with the breath of God's own world.

Her body animated by the same divine breath
that raised Adam from dust
and would one day raise dry bones to life.

> "I will cause breath to enter you,
> and you will live."
> —Ezekiel 37:5

Her eyes opening into the face of the One who already knew:

every contour of her body,
every nuance of her personality,
every dimension of her strength,
every shade of her softness.

Before she ever heard Adam speak,
she heard God's delight.

Before she ever felt the weight of expectation,
she felt the warmth of divine approval.

Before shame existed,
she existed beloved.

Why?
Because the first voice that told her who she was
was the voice of her Creator.

Yeshua—who would one day breathe peace over fearful
disciples—was the same One who breathed identity into Eve.

> "He breathed on them and said,
> 'Receive the Holy Spirit.'"
> —John 20:22

Her identity was not assembled from opinions,
performance,
perfectionism,
comparison,
or culture.

Her identity was carved from holy love.

She began whole.
Radiant.
Rooted.
Secure.

And that knowing held her.
Like air.
Like light.
Like breath.

Before she ever knew hiding,
she knew being fully seen.
Before she was named by Adam,
she was named by God.

Before Eve heard a word from anyone,
she inhaled the delight of her Maker.

> "Lord, You have searched me and known me."
> —Psalm 139:1

Before the fracture,
there was only a woman
held in the gaze of her Maker
with no need to be anything
but who He had formed her to be.

Have you ever wondered what your life would feel like if God's
voice—
not expectation,
not memory,
not comparison—
was the first voice you heard?

Before Eve ever heard a human voice, she heard God's delight.

Eve's Second Relationship: Herself
And Yours, Too

After Eve opened her eyes to the face of God,
after she breathed in the atmosphere of perfect love,
something sacred happened inside her:

She became a woman who could live peacefully with herself.
And this is the invitation for you, too.

Self here doesn't mean selfishness;
it means the woman God created you to be—
known, held, and at peace within.

Before she ever met Adam—
whether that was moments after her creation or days later,
we aren't told—
Eve existed in a world where only she and God breathed the
same air.

Scripture invites us to imagine what that must have been like:

A woman walking through the Garden
with an internal rest most modern women don't even know how
to imagine . . .

She walked in the cool of the day, unhurried, unpressured,
unworried.
She explored creation with curiosity instead of self-
consciousness.

We are picturing something the Bible doesn't describe in detail—
but it's a picture consistent with everything Scripture tells us
about God's goodness and humanity's original innocence.

Scripture gives us three words that hold an entire universe:

Naked and unashamed.

We rush past it,
but Eve *lived* it.

Three words, but they open a window into a world we can
scarcely imagine.

If we let those words speak . . .

She lived in a body she did not criticize.
She lived in emotions she did not second-guess.
She lived in desires she did not hide.
She lived in a soul that felt no pressure to perform,
compete, or compare.

We are reading between the lines here—
but the lines themselves invite it.

The text doesn't describe Eve's psychology,
but it tells us something just as important:

in the beginning,
before the fracture,
there was no shame.
No hiding.
No self-protection.
Only freedom.
Only peace.
Only being fully known and fully unafraid.

She was simply—
herself.
Fully.
Freely.
Joyfully.

And here is the part we rarely consider:

Eve didn't wonder who she was supposed to be.

She had no mirrors.
No filtered images.
No comparison culture.
No insecurity.
No constant commentary about her body, her worth, or her place.

She did not look over her shoulder to see if someone else was doing it better.
She didn't shrink to stay likable.
She didn't apologize for taking up space.
She didn't adjust her personality to stay acceptable.

Why?

A question many women ask in reverse:

Why am I performing? Why am I always shrinking?

She knew who she was because she was known.

God's voice was the first voice she heard.
God's delight was the first delight she felt.
God's presence was the first presence she experienced.

And because she was deeply, wholly, overwhelmingly seen,
she could live deeply, wholly, overwhelmingly **as herself**.

Her femininity wasn't a liability.
Her emotions weren't too much.
Her intuition wasn't dismissed.
Her tenderness wasn't mocked.
Her strength wasn't threatening.
Her beauty wasn't weaponized.
Her desire for connection wasn't used against her.

Eve carried none of the internal tension we carry now.

She walked in the cool of the day, unhurried, unpressured, unworried.
She explored creation with curiosity

instead of self-consciousness.
She named what she felt without fear of judgment.
She showed up exactly as she was—
because she knew she was already enough.

We don't know what tasks she performed in those early moments, but we do know this:

Whatever she did,
she did without doubting herself.
Without apology.
Without striving.
Without fear that she would disappoint someone.

She was a woman whose internal world was whole.

Imagine that kind of freedom.

Can you imagine waking up with no voice in your mind telling you to:

try harder . . .
be quieter . . .
be smaller . . .
be prettier . . .
be thinner . . .
be less emotional . . .
be more put-together . . .
or be anything other than the woman God made you to be?

That is the kind of freedom Eve likely knew.
Because Eve's identity came directly from the One who designed her.

Here is the truth Scripture whispers:

The same **God** who **formed Eve formed you.**
The same **God** who **delighted** in **Eve delights in you.**
The same **blessing** spoken over **creation**, *very good*, rests over **your life** too.

Radiance is not earned.
It is remembered.

And it begins where Eve began,
with God's breath.

Only when a woman is held by God can she finally rest in her
own skin and love from overflow, not longing.

As you imagine Eve walking in the freedom of being fully
herself—seen, known, unashamed—
where do you sense your own soul longing to return to that kind
of wholeness?

Wholeness always begins with God,
but it never ends there.

When a woman is grounded in being fully seen by her Creator,
she becomes a woman who can live peacefully within herself.

And only then—**only from that place of internal rest—**
is she ready to encounter another.

Eve did not come to Adam searching for identity.
She came bearing one.

She did not arrive hoping to be chosen.
She arrived already delighted in.

She did not stand before him wondering who she needed to
become.
She stood before him already whole.

And so when God brought her to Adam,
it wasn't to complete her—
it was to *recognize* her.

It is here, in this sacred sequence—

God → Yourself → Others—

that we step into Eve's third relationship.

A relationship not built on grasping,
but on overflow.
Not on fear,
but on rest.
Not on identity seeking,
but on identity sharing.

Eve's Third Relationship: Adam

Eve did not come to Adam looking for herself—
she came already found.

Only after Eve knew God,
and only after she lived at peace within herself,
did God bring her to Adam.

The sequence was intentional.
The order was protective.
The timing was holy.

And when Adam saw her,
he didn't define her—
he recognized her.

> "This one, at last, is bone of my bone
> and flesh of my flesh."
> —Genesis 2:23

He spoke what God had already declared:

strong helper,
warrior ally,
equal partner,

counterpart,
co-ruler.

The Hebrew word is *ezer*[1]—
a word most women have never been taught,
and one that has been quietly misunderstood.

Ezer does not mean *assistant*.

It appears throughout the Old Testament,
often in significant contexts.

The same word describes God Himself when He comes to Israel's
aid as deliverer, protector and strength.

It describes military allies coming to each other's support.
Sometimes it even describes help that fails or disappoints—
but in Eden, there is no failure,
only fit.

The point is this:

Ezer is a word of dignity.
It names someone who supplies what another lacks.

Not an afterthought.
Not decoration.
Not a subordinate.

But **divine reinforcement**
for the work of tending and protecting
and loving God's world.

She was essential—
an ally, a counterpart,
a strength Adam did not possess alone.

She was, as the text says,
bone of his bone and flesh of his flesh—
equal in essence, unique in design, united in purpose.

She came to Adam whole—
not hoping he would make her so.

What would your relationships look like
if you lived from wholeness
instead of hoping someone else could give it to you?

I once sat with a woman who whispered,
almost embarrassed,
I don't know who I am without people needing me.

After a long pause, she added,
*I don't think I've ever known myself
outside of what I do.*

Her words carried generations of women's stories:

the performing,
the proving,
the disappearing.

When I told her gently,
Before you ever did anything . . . God saw you.
Before anyone expected anything of you . . . God named you,
her tears came—not from pain,
but from recognition.

From remembering.

She wiped her face and said softly,
Something in me has always known that.

Of course it did.
Eden lives inside us.
We are simply learning to hear it again.

Eve shows us the way home:

God → Yourself → Others

Identity from God.
Security within ourselves.
Relationships flowing not from desperation,
but from overflow.

Centuries later,
Jesus echoed the same rhythm:

> "Love your neighbor as yourself."
> —Mark 12:31

We often rush past the second part.
Jesus didn't.

You cannot love others well
if you do not know the love of the Father.
You cannot pour compassion
if you have never received it.
You cannot offer tenderness
if you have never been allowed to feel your own.
You cannot love your neighbor
if you do not know how to love the woman God created in you.

And you cannot love yourself rightly
until you know the God who named you,
formed you,
delights in you,
and calls you His own.

Eve lived from that divine order.
We were designed for that divine order.
And every fracture in a woman's story
begins the moment that order gets reversed.

God → Yourself → Others

That's the only order in which identity stays intact.

This pattern echoes what Jesus would later call the greatest commandment:

love God,
love your neighbor as yourself.
The order matters—
but so does the harmony.

These loves are not a ladder we climb one rung at a time,
never looking back.

They are more like a rhythm we learn to breathe:

held by God,
at home with ourselves,
free to love others from wholeness rather than hunger.

But here is the hope
woven through Scripture
and through your own breath:

What God establishes, He **restores.**
What the world distorts, He **renames.**
What shame buries, He **resurrects.**

As we move into the next chapter,
we begin exploring the first cracks in that divine order—
the quiet messages that taught us to hide,
to hustle,
to perform,
to disappear,
and to forget the girl God placed in us
before the world tried to rewrite her.

Where have you forgotten the woman God designed you to be—
and what might it feel like to return to her?

Wholeness is not something another person gives you.
It is what God restores in you
so you can love without losing yourself.

Eve began this way—
whole,
held,
and at rest in God's presence.

Her first breath was peace.
Her first gaze was not toward another human,
but toward God.

As we turn the page, we step into the tension every woman
eventually encounters—
the place where the world's messages begin competing with
God's design.

Somewhere between girlhood and womanhood,
between innocence and expectation,
between the desire to belong
and the fear of disappointing others,
we begin to hear other voices.

Quieter at first.
Then louder.
Then so familiar we mistake them for truth.

We are not naming these places to bring you shame.
We are naming them with gentleness so you can understand
what shaped you and move forward with freedom.

Because every fracture has a beginning—
and every restoration begins with remembering what was true
before the fracture ever came.

PART II

FRACTURE AND SURVIVAL

How radiance dims,
then breaks — without
shame.

Chapter 3

WHEN RADIANCE
BEGAN TO FRACTURE

How life begins to teach a girl to disappear.

The Quiet Beginning

There is a moment—
often quiet,
often ordinary,
rarely dramatic—
when a girl first realizes
the world has opinions about who she should be.

Not in a single event.
Not in a moment she could easily point to.

But in the slow accumulation of messages—
subtle enough to dismiss,
steady enough to shape her.

No girl wakes up one morning and decides to forget herself.
She learns.
She adjusts.
She adapts.

And often, she does it without realizing anything has been lost.

If this already feels familiar, take a breath.
You are not behind.
You are not late.
You are simply noticing.

Before any woman learns to shrink,
before she learns to adjust herself,
before she learns to make others comfortable
at the expense of her own soul,
there is usually a moment.

Small in appearance.
Lasting in impact.

A moment when radiance meets resistance.
When innocence meets interpretation.
When the girl God placed in her begins to sense—
often without words—
that being herself may come at a cost.

Some women remember this moment clearly.
Others only feel its echo.

But most of us learned, in one way or another,
that our unfiltered self was
too bright,
too soft,
too loud,
too emotional,
too much—
or not enough.

As you read, I want to say this gently and clearly:

You are not required to remember everything.
You are not asked to feel everything.
You are not expected to locate a defining moment.

Some women recognize their story immediately.
Others only feel a soft tug—
a sense that something here matters.
Both are enough.

We are not opening old wounds to re-enter pain.
We are noticing patterns with kindness,
so the girl inside you does not feel alone anymore.

The First Fracture: A Different Voice

Scripture gives language to this moment.

Eden was whole—
until one conversation introduced confusion.

The serpent did not approach Eve because she was weak.
In Eden, what was targeted was not weakness, but design—
her relational strength,
her radiance.

The enemy has always known:

distort the woman's identity,
and the design begins to unravel.

In Eden, the serpent did not begin with behavior.
The serpent began with a question.

> *"Did God really say . . . ?"*
> —Genesis 3:1

With that whisper, something shifted—
not in Eve's worth,
but in the clarity of the voice she trusted.

Once God's voice became blurry,
everything else became vulnerable.

Then came the second distortion:

You will be like God.

But she already was.

She bore His image.
She carried His likeness.
She embodied His creativity, authority, and beauty.

The lie was not that she could become more—
the lie was that she lacked what she already possessed.

And this tactic has never changed.

The enemy convinces women to strive
for what God already placed inside them.
Let this land gently.
This is not about blame.
It is about understanding.

When Shame Is Born

Scripture tells us their eyes were opened.
Not to wonder.
Not to glory.
But to self-consciousness.

The world that once felt safe
now felt threatening.

The bodies they once inhabited with ease
now felt exposed.

And so they hid.

They stitched fig leaves together—
the first coping mechanism,
the first performance,
the first mask.

Shame entered not as punishment,
but as disorientation.

And God came walking.

Not rushing.
Not thundering.
Walking.

And He asked a question that still echoes through women's hearts:

Where are you?

Not because He had lost them—
but because they had lost themselves.

Shame is not simply feeling bad.
Shame is the moment a woman stops recognizing
the radiant girl God created,
and begins searching for a safer version of herself.

The Fracture in Our Own Stories

We often think shame arrives later—
after betrayal,
after heartbreak,
after failure.

But shame usually comes much earlier.
Quietly.
Politely.
In places that were meant to feel safe.

Classrooms.
Church pews.
Living rooms.
Kitchen tables.
Ball fields.

Sometimes through sharp words.
More often through unguarded moments
from people who loved us
but didn't know how to hold our hearts.

A sigh.
A comparison.

A rule that felt too heavy.
A silence that lingered too long.
The world calls these things *small.*
But a girl's heart does not experience them as small.

Because a girl's heart is still forming.
Still open.

Still learning who she is allowed to be.

If you feel yourself remembering now,
you do not need to go faster.
You are safe to stay right here.

The Second-Grade Moment That Taught Me to Hide

I was a Tigger girl from the beginning—
bouncy, chatty, full of movement and curiosity,
a storm of sunshine with absolutely no idea what to do with all
that energy.

I didn't fit neatly into quiet rows or silent sanctuaries.

Stillness was something adults wanted from me,
not something my body knew how to offer.

One afternoon in Mrs. Moody's second-grade classroom,
I put on my first fig leaf.

The day felt tight from the start—
the kind of day where the air in the room feels heavy
and the teacher's patience sits right at the surface.

She raised her voice—rare for her—and declared,
The next person who speaks will go to the office.

A hush fell across the room.

But inside me
was a storm of held-back energy
and a heart that always, instinctively, rose up for justice.

Ben, the boy next to me, reached over and stole my crayons—
right off my desk.

It was small.
It was silly.

But it was injustice to my little heart.

And I fired before I aimed.
Give me my crayons back!

The second the words left my mouth,
I knew.

Before she even spoke,
I felt Mrs. Moody's glare
tighten the air around my body.

Heat crawled up my cheeks.

Shame—
before I even knew that word—
settled inside me.

She marched me down the hallway,
my breath catching in my throat,
my heart pounding like it was trying to outrun the moment.

I knew what this meant—
if you get in trouble at school,
you get in more trouble at home.

The principal's office swallowed me whole:

the lecture,
the scowl,
the note to take home,
adult disappointment written across every face . . .

And the spanking that followed.

As I sat alone in my room afterward,
I learned a lesson I would carry for years:

Part of me is too much.
I need to adjust who I am.
My voice creates trouble.
Better to hold it in next time.

That was the day I stitched my first fig leaf.

And the fracture began.

The Girl on My Couch

Years later, a young woman sat across from me.

I don't know who I am without trying to be what everyone else needs.

She traced it back to nine years old.

Reading her mother's moods.
Adjusting her presence.
Learning to disappear.

She hadn't been abused.
She had just been needed.

And somewhere in that needing, she learned:

My presence matters most when I don't need anything.

Her hiding was not rebellion.
It was survival.

Every woman I have ever counseled
has some version of this moment.

Different details.
Same outcome.

The radiant girl becomes the responsible one.
The expressive one becomes the agreeable one.
The whole one becomes a managed version of herself.

When Girls Begin to Hide

Every woman has her own second-grade moment.

It may not look the same as mine—
maybe hers came through a parent's sharp criticism,
a church that prized good behavior over honest hearts,
a friend who betrayed her trust,
a sibling she was constantly compared to,
a coach who mistook tenderness for weakness,
a teacher whose impatience landed on her like shame,
a boy who laughed at something sacred inside her,
or the quiet ache of a home where no one knew how to hold her
emotions.

But the impact is the same:

The radiant girl becomes the *responsible* one.
The imaginative one becomes the *quiet* one.

The expressive one becomes the *agreeable* one.
The brave one becomes the *good* one.
The whole one becomes the half version of herself.
And without realizing it,
she begins to live out the same inverted order Eve experienced:

Others → Yourself → God.

What do they need from me?
How do I make them happy?
Where should I shrink?
What part of myself is too much?
Who do I need to become so no one is disappointed?

The girl disappears.

And the performer rises.
She learns to scan the room before she speaks.
She learns to measure her worth by other people's moods.
She learns to trade authenticity for acceptance.
She learns to survive by becoming agreeable, adaptable,
accommodating.

Not because she is weak—
but because somewhere along the way,
her heart absorbed a quiet lie:

The real me is risky.

And most of the time,
that lesson begins much earlier than we think.
Not in adulthood,
but in girlhood—
when radiance learns to make itself small.

Hiding begins the moment a girl decides that who she truly is
might cost her too much.

The Universal Messages

Girls everywhere absorb the same quiet commandments:

Be small.
Be polite.
Be good.
Be easy.

Be strong—
but not too strong.
Be soft—
but not too soft.

They sound harmless.
But over time,
they become fig leaves.

And so hiding begins.

Women don't lose their radiance.
They learn which parts of it the world will allow.
Not because she was wrong—
but because the world didn't know how to hold her.

God's Gentle Voice in Our Hiding

And yet—
Eden offers one more truth.

Even after we hide, God does not withdraw.

After the fall,
after the hiding,
after the fig leaves,
after the fear,
after shame rewrote the story Eve once knew by heart . . .
God came walking.

Not rushing.
Not roaring.
Not thundering.

Walking.

The sound of footsteps in the cool of the day—
the same sound Eve once associated with peace—
was now echoing through a world freshly fractured.

And still,
God called out.

Not with condemnation,
but with invitation:

Where are you?

He was not angry—
He was seeking.

He was not accusing—
He was restoring.

He was not exposing to humiliate—
He was revealing to heal.

Because God has never lost track of you—
even on the days you've lost track of yourself.

He still walks toward women who hide.
He still seeks daughters who've forgotten their radiance.
He still calls us out of the shadows with a tenderness—
the kind that refuses to shame us for needing rescue.

God's first question to humanity wasn't,
What have you done?

It was, *Where are you?*—
because His desire has always been to **find you**,
not to fault you.

So as you pause for a moment,
let your heart breathe and consider:

Where did you begin to hide,
and what might it feel like to let God walk toward you again—
not to expose your shame,
but to restore your radiance?

Because every woman has her own fig-leaf moment.
Not always loud,
not always obvious,
but real.

A moment she stopped trusting her voice.
A moment she traded radiance for approval.
A moment she learned to shrink while the world kept
demanding more.

And often, the fracture didn't start in adulthood—
it started in a little girl's heart.

A Moment for Your Own Heart

If you were to trace your story back—
before the disappointments,
before the heartbreak,
before the hard years,
before the divorce,
before the quiet surviving—
you would find her.

A younger you.
A tender you.
A radiant you.

A girl who learned a lesson that did not come from God.

A moment—
often small,
often forgotten—
when she absorbed a message she was never meant to carry:

Maybe I should be quieter.
Maybe I should be easier.
Maybe I should hide this part of me.
Maybe the real me is risky.

She didn't learn these ideas from Eden.
She learned them from the ache of a world that didn't know how
to hold her.

And here is the tender truth:

your heart will remember that moment
long before your mind does.

It's the moment your radiance first stepped back.
The moment your voice softened into hesitation.
The moment the girl God delighted in began to question her
own goodness.

So take a breath.

Let your body settle.

And gently ask your own heart:

When did I first begin to hide?
And what did I believe about myself at that moment?

Somewhere in every woman's story
there is a moment she began to hide—
not because she was wrong,
but because the world was not ready for her radiance.

And once a girl begins to hide,
something integral shifts inside her.

Not all at once.
Not loudly.

But quietly—
the way light dims before a storm.

Because hiding doesn't stay small.
It becomes a pattern,
a posture,
a way of moving through the world.

And slowly,
without realizing it,
the girl God formed in radiance
starts living from a place of self-protection.

Which brings us to the next truth every woman must eventually face:

Hiding always grows roots.
And those roots shape the woman she becomes.

Let's step into that together.

The Invitation: God Finds Us Before We Find Ourselves

If God's question reveals His heart, the invitation reveals ours.

Just as He walked toward Eve in the garden,
God has always been the God who comes close after the fracture.

He does not shame women for their hiding—
He seeks them in it.

And He still asks the same question:

Where are you?

Not to expose you—
but to restore you.
Not to punish you—
but to bring you home
to the radiance that was never lost,
only buried.

The girl God placed inside you is not gone.

She is waiting—
beneath the performance,
beneath the pleasing,
beneath the fear,
beneath the armor.

And naming the fracture
is the first step toward remembering
who you've always been.

So take these questions slowly.
You don't have to answer all of them.
Let one question choose you.

Can you remember a moment—
childhood or adolescence—
when you first felt the pressure to be good,
quiet, strong,
or easy?

A moment where you realized—
without anyone saying it—
that being fully yourself might cost something?

What early messages shaped the way you moved through the
world?

The unspoken commandments like:

Don't need too much.
Don't take up space.
Don't be emotional.
Be perfect.
Be agreeable.
Make everyone comfortable.

Which of these messages still cling to your heart?
Was there a time when you were loved . . .
but not truly seen?

How did you adjust yourself to remain acceptable,
likable,
peaceful?

And what would it feel like for that younger version of you to
finally exhale?

What does your heart long to unlearn?
And even more—
what does it long to remember?

God still calls the hiding heart.

> "So the Lord God called out to the man
> and said to him,
> *'Where are you?'"*
> —Genesis 3:9

> "Return to your rest, my soul,
> for the LORD has been good to you."
> —Psalm 116:7

Because the fracture wasn't your fault,
and returning to yourself isn't rebellion—
it's restoration.

I pray that God gently brings to mind
the moments that shaped you—
not to wound you,
but to free you.

And I pray you begin recognizing the exact places where your
radiance dimmed . . .
so you can reclaim the girl God placed within you long before
the world told you who to be.

Hiding may have kept you safe once,
but it cannot lead you home.

Only truth can do that—
and God meets you in both.

Take a breath.

You do not need to remember everything.
Just notice.

Because naming the fracture is not the end of the story.

It is the beginning of remembering who you were
before the world taught you to disappear.

And that is where the journey of coming home begins.

Chapter 4

WHERE RADIANCE BREAKS

---

*Some breaks don't shatter you;
they reveal the woman you
were always meant to become.*

Before we go any further, let me say this gently:

not every fracture announces itself as a breaking.

Some fractures live quietly for years,
shaping how a woman carries strength, love, responsibility, and silence.

What you are about to read is not the beginning of my story,
but the moment the earlier fractures could no longer stay hidden.

At thirty-one, the world did not simply shift beneath me—
it ruptured.

Betrayal has a sound.

Mine was the soft, devastating confession:

Yes . . . I did,
followed by the quiet click of a door closing behind me.

And then—silence.

But not the peaceful kind.
The kind that echoes in your bones.

It was Christmas.

The house was glowing with white lights.
The Sound of Music humming in the background,
and the scent of our fresh Fraser fir drifting through the living
room.

There were ornaments my children had hung a little crooked,
stockings my mother had made,
little fingerprints smudged across the windows,
and a half-finished gingerbread house hardening on the counter,
with remnants of wrapping paper still tucked under the sofa.

It looked like a home overflowing with joy.
It felt like a place where something holy had just shattered.

At the time, I had four little ones:

a six-year-old, a four-year-old, a two-year-old,
and a six-month-old baby still nursing.

I can still picture where each one was in the house that night:

the baby swing rocking in the corner,
tiny shoes lined up neatly by the front door,
a pacifier drying on a towel beside the sink—
ordinary snapshots of a life I loved . . .
and a life I suddenly wasn't sure how to hold together.

Here is the part no one tells you:

betrayal often doesn't wait for a quiet season.

It comes when your arms are full,
your heart is open,
your body is tired,
your attention is divided,
your hope is high,
or your life is already stretched thin.

It comes during pregnancy,
during the holidays,
during caregiving seasons,
during milestone moments,
during anniversaries,
during new beginnings,
or right after a woman has poured herself out
emotionally, physically, spiritually.

So many women think:

How could this happen now?
Of all times . . . why during this?
Why when I was trying so hard?
Why when I needed him most?

Because betrayal doesn't just break trust.

It breaks **timing.**
It ruptures the very moment you thought was safe.
It ambushes you in the middle of love,
of giving,
of being the best version of yourself
you know how to be.

When betrayal enters a story,
it doesn't just wound the heart—
it disorients the soul.

It reverses the divine order—
what was meant to be shelter,
becomes a threat.

And a woman who once breathed freely finds herself gasping for
air.

I sank to the floor before my mind could catch up to my body.

My knees hit the carpet,
my hands met the earth,
and for a moment, I couldn't breathe—
as if the weight of truth had pressed the air right out of my
lungs.

There are moments that divide a woman's life
into **before**
and **after.**

This was mine.

To understand why that night broke me the way it did,
I have to take you back—
not to drama,
but to formation.

But like every woman who has ever found herself on the floor,
breath stolen by a truth she never asked to hold,
my story didn't begin in the breaking.

It began with a girl full of wonder.

Before the Fracture

Before everything broke at thirty-one,
there was a girl becoming a woman—
slowly, quietly, beautifully—
with no idea that the earliest cracks in her radiance
were already beginning to form.

At eighteen,
I arrived at Samford University from Florida with my twin sister—
two girls stepping into adulthood
with wide eyes and the kind of wonder
held only by those who haven't yet tasted disappointment.

I was eight hours from home,
eight hours from the rules that shaped me,
and for the first time in a long time,
I felt like I could breathe.

A Christian campus gave me the framework to flourish;
I didn't have to rebel to find space—
I simply had room.

Room to imagine.
To grow.
To become.
To feel the sun on my face
without wondering if I was too much of anything.

College felt full of promise,
late-night conversations in hallways,
friendships forged over cafeteria tables,
dreams spoken out loud with the kind of innocence
you only get once.

There were unlimited possibilities,
a sense of calling,
and the gentle unfolding of a young woman finding her way.

At twenty, I met the man I believed would be my forever.
At twenty-two, I walked down the aisle,
heart steady, eyes bright,
believing love would be enough to hold us both.

At twenty-five, I became a mother,
and something deep in me softened,

opened,
expanded,
in a holy way I didn't know was possible.

Those early years held sweetness,
the kind of tenderness you don't fully appreciate
until life gives you a reason to miss it.

There were bedtime stories,
new-mama wonder,
tiny hands reaching for mine,
quiet mornings where everything felt whole.

But even in the sweetness,
something else was forming beneath the surface—
not brokenness, not yet,
but the beginning shape of it.

Woven into those years
were seeds I didn't know I was planting.
Subtle ones.
Silent ones.
Seeds that would later grow into the quiet fractures of my soul.

I was becoming:

the dependable one,
the steady one,
the capable one,
the girl who could absorb disappointment
without letting it break the surface.

I didn't know that strength—
untethered from vulnerability—
slowly becomes armor.

I didn't know that being the strong one
often means being the silent one.

Most women don't notice when it begins.
I didn't either.

Because the fracture always begins
long before the breaking.

Strength without vulnerability feels noble—
until it becomes the armor that keeps us from being known.

Looking back, I can see that the breaking at thirty-one wasn't the
beginning—but the unveiling.

Where Radiance First Dimmed

My sophomore year, something happened that I wouldn't
understand until much later.

I had been singing with Samford's elite A Cappella Choir,
and that spring we were preparing for a tour through Europe—
cathedrals, concert halls, once-in-a-lifetime opportunities.
It was the kind of thing a college girl dreams about.

At the same time, I felt drawn to something different:

Beach Project—
a summer ministry on the Gulf Coast
that stirred something alive and hopeful in me.

It felt like God.
Like freedom.
Like my own choice.

Growing up on the water,
the intercoastal waterway and the beach had always been more
than a place.

They were where I first learned to hear God.
Where the rhythm of the waves quieted my mind.

Where I prayed without knowing I was praying.
Where beauty felt like belonging.

So when Beach Project opened up,
my heart leapt.
It felt like an invitation into a deeper part of myself—
a place where God and I had always met.
I went to my A Cappella Choir director to tell him I wouldn't be
able to tour.

What happened next
is the kind of moment that shapes a girl quietly—
not through violence,
but through dismissal.

He didn't just discourage me.
He called my pastor.
And my father.

Three men making a decision for me
about my future,
my calling,
my desires,
my voice.

No one asked what I wanted.
No one asked where God was stirring.
No one asked why the beach felt like home
or why ministry felt like purpose.

My voice didn't matter.
My decision was handled behind closed doors
by people who loved me
but didn't see me.

And yet Scripture tells us of a God who sees the unseen woman:

> "So she named the Lord who spoke her:
> 'You are El-roi,' for she said, 'In this place,
> have I actually seen the one who sees me?'"
> —Genesis 16:13

But in that moment,
something in me learned:

Shrink back.
Behave.
Be compliant.
Your voice is too small to matter.

It was a tiny fracture—
subtle, almost invisible—
but it taught me something
I would carry for years:

You can want something deeply
and still not choose it.
You can know something is right for you
and still surrender it . . .
because someone else knows better.

I didn't know it then, but that moment planted a belief in me
that would shape every part of my marriage and adulthood:

I will absorb this.
I will adjust.
I will not make it a problem.

It was the beginning of losing myself in the name of peace.
The beginning of disappearing in the name of harmony.
The beginning of radiance shifting into responsibility.

Because the breaking is just the final straw;
the fracture began long before anyone noticed.

As you look back on your own story,
can you name one early moment—
small or subtle—
when you first learned to shrink, adjust,
or quiet yourself to keep the peace?

What did that moment teach you about your worth . . .
and what might God be gently un-teaching now?

You don't have to answer everything today.
Just notice what rises.
And let that be enough.

> "Because you are precious in my sight,
> and honored, and I love you."
> —Isaiah 43:4

This verse doesn't rush you.
This verse doesn't shame you.
This verse simply sits beside you in the place where radiance first cracked.

I pray that you feel the nearness of the God who sees you,
who gathers every unshed tear and every unspoken thought.

And may this be the beginning of learning to breathe again—
not as the woman the world required you to be,
but as the woman God delighted to create.

**You can be loved and still unseen—
but God never confuses the two.**

And as the light begins to touch the places where your radiance
first dimmed,
there is a gentler work He is already beginning in you—
a returning to the parts of yourself you slowly learned to forget.

Forgetting doesn't always feel like a wound.
Sometimes it feels like becoming responsible,
or strong,
or easy to love.

But beneath those layers is a girl who once lived open, bright,
and unafraid—
and God is ready to help you remember her.

What comes next is tender terrain:

not the moment you first hid,
but the long, quiet years when hiding became ordinary.

Come gently.

You are not walking into **shame**—
but into **remembrance**.

Chapter 5

FORGETTING HER RADIANCE

What the soul learns when love feels uncertain.

Forgetting begins when a girl learns—
slowly,
quietly—
how to survive in a world that does not always know how to
hold her tenderness.

Radiance is *not* fragile.
But it *is* responsive.

And what rises in you now may be remembering.

When love feels uncertain, radiance learns to guard.
When presence feels inconsistent, radiance learns to manage.
When safety is shaken, radiance learns to organize life around
protection.

Nothing here means something went wrong with you.
It means something *happened* to you.

Before we name anything further, I want you to know this:

You do not need to recognize yourself in every word.
You do not need to remember everything.
You do not need to feel anything deeply today.
You are free to simply notice—gently, honestly, without pressure.

This chapter is not an examination.

It is an invitation to curiosity.

> "Do not fear, for I have redeemed you;
> I have called you by your name; you are mine."
> —Isaiah 43:1

Radiance Was Never Lost—It Learned to Hide

No girl is born disconnected from her radiance.

Little girls arrive twirling—
skirts spinning,
bare feet slapping against warm earth,
imaginations spilling through their fingertips
as if heaven pressed creativity straight into their palms.

I'm reminding you of this because when we name survival
patterns, shame will try to convince you that you were *born this way*.

You weren't.
You adapted.

Girls believe—
deep down—
that they are meant to delight and be delighted in.

They believe they are safe.

They believe the world has room
for their voice,
their joy,

their emotions,
their God-given complexity.

But over time,
through a slow accumulation of *small moments*—
sharp words,
conditional love,
inconsistency,
and a world that praises composure and overlooks the heart—
she learns what costs less—
and what costs too much.

It's safer to please.
It's necessary to perform.
It's costly to need.

These messages do not arrive like hurricanes.

They settle like dust—
dust on dreams,
dust on desire,
dust on identity.

And quietly,
faithfully,
radiance goes underground—
not because she is weak,
but because she is trying to survive.

> "Why, my soul, are you so dejected?
> Why are you in such turmoil?"
> —Psalm 42:5

So we come into the light slowly—held, not hurried.

What follows are not diagnoses, but common shapes radiance
takes when love feels uncertain.

Grit helped you survive.
Grace is what helps you soften without fear.

Seven Ways Radiance Learned to Protect Itself

As a woman's radiance encounters a world that cannot
consistently hold her, her soul does not disappear.

It compensates.
It organizes.
It survives.

The patterns that emerge are not personality flaws.
They are the shape radiance took in order to stay alive.

As you read, notice what whispers, not what shouts.
If something doesn't fit, let it pass.
Nothing here needs to be claimed.

1. When Radiance Learned to Stay Alert

Some women notice they live with a quiet vigilance—
always scanning, preparing, bracing.

This does not mean you are anxious by nature.
It means your nervous system learned early that safety could not
be assumed.

When protection was inconsistent,
radiance learned to become its own guardian.

This was not failure.
It was wisdom—
formed too young,
held too long.

2. When Radiance Learned to Earn

Others notice they work hard to be chosen,
approved, or valued—even by God.

When love feels conditional,
radiance learns to strive for what was meant to be freely given.
Striving is not pride.
It is the hope that if she does enough, love will stay.

3. When Radiance Learned to Disappear

Some of us notice our desires went quiet over time.

When her needs were dismissed or overlooked,
radiance learned that wanting felt unsafe.

So she learned to echo others instead of listening inward.

This was not self-neglect.
It was self-preservation.

The Woman Who Disappeared Without Leaving

I once sat with a woman who quietly said,
I haven't had a desire of my own in years.

She wasn't depressed.
She wasn't rebellious.
She had simply gone missing.

Decision by decision,
year by year,
she had folded herself into the shape of what her life required—
quiet, agreeable, accommodating.

Nothing dramatic happened.
No single moment marked her disappearance.

One day, she realized she could not remember the last time she
said the words,
I want . . .

Not because she didn't care.
But because wanting had stopped feeling safe.

She didn't need rebellion.
She didn't need to be told to take her life back.

She needed permission to remember.
She needed resurrection—
gentle, unforced, and held.

If any part of this feels familiar, notice it kindly.
There is no rush.

There are other ways radiance learned to stay safe, too.

4. When Radiance Learned to Hold Everything Together

You may notice you became the steady one—
emotionally, mentally, spiritually.

When responsibility outweighed support,
radiance learned to carry what should have been shared.

Strength grew where softness once lived.
And for a time, it worked.

5. When Radiance Learned to Shut Down

You may notice moments of numbness,
withdrawal, or collapse.

When the cost of staying strong became unbearable,
radiance learned to cope by going quiet.

This is not weakness.
It is the body asking for mercy.

6. When Radiance Learned to Be Consumed

Others notice they pour out endlessly but rarely feel poured into.

When giving became the only way to belong,
radiance forgot she was never meant to be used up.

Being consumed is not love.
It is depletion.

7. When Radiance Learned to Disconnect

Some of us notice distance—
from our body, our joy, our voice, even from God.

This is not rebellion.
It is exhaustion.

When rest never arrived, radiance learned to drift.

These are not failures.
They are survival strategies—
the ways a radiant soul learned to live in a world that did not yet
know how to hold her.

But here is the truth I want you to hear gently:

Survival patterns can protect you—
but they cannot restore you.

And they were never meant to be permanent.

"But I will bring you health and heal you of your
wounds—this is the Lord's declaration."
—Jeremiah 30:17

A Gentle Remembering, Not a Condemnation

If something stirred as you read—
a heaviness,
a quiet ache,
a recognition without words—that is not shame.

That is remembrance.

God never reveals a wound without already preparing a place for healing.

You are not being exposed.
You are being understood.

And understanding is the beginning of safety.

Before we go any further, take a breath.
You do not need to do anything with what you noticed here.

No fixing.
No sorting.
No deciding.
Just presence.

You might gently ask your heart—not to answer, just to notice:

Where did I first learn to protect myself?
What patterns once helped me survive?
What parts of me feel tired, not broken?

Let those questions rest.
They are not assignments.
They are invitations.

> "Come to Me,
> all of you who are weary and burdened,
> and I will give you rest."
> —Matthew 11:28

Radiance that went underground did not disappear.
It waited.

And now, slowly, kindly, God is inviting you back—
not to perform healing,
but to be held.

Where We Go Next

Before God restores identity,
He restores a sense of safety.
Before He tells you who you are,
He teaches your body what it feels like to be safe enough to listen.

The next chapter is not about examining failures.
It is about meeting the God
who steps into the places where care for you fell short,
who steadies what was never stabilized,
and who re-parents what was overwhelmed.

You will not be asked to rush grief.
You will not be asked to fix your story.
You will be invited to rest.

PART III

RECEIVING WHAT WAS MISSING

Care, presence, protection—and the love that stays.

Chapter 6

THE MOTHER WOUND: WILL I BE CARED FOR?

*Where our need for care was formed—
and where God meets it.*

Read with compassion, not investigation.
Curiosity is a form of gentleness.

Beneath so much of what we carry, one question remains:

Will I be cared for?

If you notice your body tightening,
your chest getting heavy,
or your mind racing, pause.

Take one slow breath.
Look around the room.
You can come back to this a little at a time.

You are not here to build a case—
you are here to name what shaped you.

Before identity is rebuilt,
safety is restored.

And for most of us, that restoration begins at the first place we
learned what care felt like:

mothering—
nurture,
provision,
presence,
and protection.

This is a question as old as human longing—
a vulnerability etched into our spirits since the Garden of Eden.

In seasons of collective fear—
like the pandemic—
this anxiety rises to the surface
and exposes something primal beneath our rational concerns.

It is not just fear of lack.
It is the soul's cry for assurance.
For abundance.
For care.
For safety.

The journey back to our feminine soul—
to our true radiance—
begins here.

Not with answers.
But with courage.

With the willingness to gently open this tender place within us . . .
and let it be named.

And when we do,
our journey inevitably leads us back . . .
back to the very first source.

To the word whispered in fever dreams of childhood,
in the loneliness of sickbeds far from home,
in the desolation of battlefields:

Mother.

Before father,
before any other relationship,
there was mother.

She was our first world.

In the womb, her body was our entire universe—
shelter, sustenance, rhythm, and warmth.

We were dependent on her in every way.
Her emotions during pregnancy—
how she felt about us,
how she felt about being pregnant—
often became the first music of our emotional life,
shaping us far beyond infancy.

In the first moments after birth,
we were placed on her chest.

Our earliest experience of attachment was with her body.
We were lifted to her breast,
and from her we received what we needed to flourish.

This isn't sentiment.
It's design.
And it's holy.

As I write this chapter,
I'm watching this reality unfold in real time.

My daughter is nursing her newborn—
my granddaughter, just weeks old.

I watch the way their bodies speak to one another without words.
The way safety passes through skin-to-skin contact.
The way nourishment flows through intimacy.

It has been impossible not to see God in it.

Breast milk itself is astonishing—
living, responsive, and beautifully designed for nourishment.

Even in the smallest amounts, its design is remarkable.

A single teaspoon contains over a million living cells.

Its composition changes throughout feeding—
foremilk to quench thirst, hindmilk to satisfy hunger—
offering care in ways that still feel wondrous to behold.

And in remarkable ways,
a mother's body responds to her baby's needs
with protection and care that feels almost beyond explanation.

Life, resilience, and immunity flow through attachment.

This was God's original design—
that our first defenses,
physically and emotionally,
would come through presence.

A Glimpse into the Sacred

A premature baby lies in an incubator,
surrounded by a quiet symphony of technology.

Tubes provide nourishment.
Monitors track heartbeats.
Every physical need is carefully attended to.

And yet something essential can still be missing.

Now imagine the mother enters.
She lifts her fragile infant and holds the baby skin-to-skin
against her chest.

And something begins to change.

The tiny body settles.
Breathing slows.
The child rests in a way machines cannot produce.

The mother's presence offers something technology cannot replicate.

And friend . . . this is a parable of the soul.

Many of us have had enough on the outside—
education, information, even religion—
but without the felt experience of attuned love,
something inside us still struggles to rest:

anxious,
shallow-breathing,
spiritually undernourished.

And this is where Jesus enters—
not as another machine,
but as *Presence*.

As anchoring, skin-to-skin love.
As the One who does not simply provide information . . .
but provides Himself.

What the Soul Learned Before Language

On an emotional level,
our deepest convictions about being cared for are often formed here:

whether we believe we will have enough care . . .
whether our needs matter . . .
whether blessing is available.

Trauma therapist Dr. Dan Allender describes this as a pre-verbal
lens formed early in life[1]—
the way we learn to make sense of ourselves,
others,
and even God.

Long before we can speak,
our nervous system is already answering:

Is the world safe?
Am I wanted?
Will I be cared for?

When a child nurses,
she drinks her fill.

Her developing soul learns something before language:

My needs matter.
I will be satisfied.
I will have enough.

But something deeper happens too.
The mother bestows what I call the benediction of being:

You are celebrated simply for being here.
Your existence brings joy.
You are a gift.

Psychiatrist Dr. Curt Thompson writes about the healing power
of being deeply seen[2]—
known and attuned to.

That gaze shapes the brain.
It shapes the body.
It shapes the soul.
To be seen is to be real.

Without a loving gaze,
the soul begins to disappear.

Resilience is born here—
not from grit, but from abundance.

From being adored.

From overwhelming care,
not scarcity.

And yet . . .

This is not everyone's story.
This chapter is not about blaming your mother.

It is about naming the climate your nervous system learned to live in.

Because what was missing still deserves to be met.

Healing does not always require confrontation.

Sometimes it begins with honest naming and receiving what God gives now.

Grit is what you learned when care was inconsistent—
how you adapted to get through.

Grace is God meeting you there now,
so you can receive and come home.

When the First World Is Unsafe

For many women,
the original blueprint was fractured.

Not always dramatically.
Sometimes quietly.

Through absence,
emotional unavailability,
and resentment instead of delight.

A mother who was overwhelmed,
depressed,
dissociated,
or wounded herself.

And I want to say this clearly:

The wound is not her personhood.

It is the climate your nervous system learned to live in.

The wound is what happens when care is inconsistent—
when presence is thin,
care feels uncertain,
and protection is not steady.

It looks like love that is warm one day and unavailable the next,
comfort that depends on mood;
a home where you don't know if your needs will be met—
or mocked.

When attuned presence is missing,
the soul learns different messages:

My needs are a burden.
Love is scarce.
I must earn care.
I must be quiet,
perfect,
or invisible to be safe.

These messages lodge deep—
shaping anxiety,
self-criticism,
and even our relationship with God.

This is where compassion must lead us—
not condemnation.

The goal is not to indict our mothers.
The goal is to understand what we are still hungry for.

And Scripture helps us do that.

Not by shaming us—
but by telling the truth gently,
so we can recognize ourselves without shame.

The Bible is not a book of perfect families.

It is a book of real stories . . .
and the God who enters them.
So let's look at a few with soft eyes.

Jacob: When Love Must Be Won

Jacob's story begins in the womb—
grasping his brother's heel, already striving.
He grows up in a home where love is divided.
His father favors Esau.
His mother favors Jacob.

And Rebecca's love is not simply tenderness—
it becomes strategy.

She schemes to secure Jacob's blessing,
and Jacob learns something about love
without anyone ever saying it out loud:

Blessing is scarce.
Love must be secured.
I must stay three steps ahead to survive.

Jacob carries this into every relationship—
including his relationship with God.

He wrestles,
bargains,
strives . . .
never quite sure of a blessing given freely.

If you learned early that love required performance,
cleverness,
or vigilance,
you may still be wrestling for what God longs to give you openly.
But Jacob's healing doesn't come through strategy.

It comes through encounter.
God meets him not as a prize to be won,
but as Presence—
the One who wounds striving and blesses becoming.

Hannah and Samuel: The Absent-Present Mother

Hannah's story is holy and heartbreaking.

After years of barrenness, she cries out for a son—
and when Samuel is born,
she gives him back to God while he is still a child.

Her devotion is sincere.
Her faith is profound.
And the cost is real.

Samuel grows up in the temple,
raised by Eli—
a well-meaning priest—tender, but too passive;
sincere, but compromised in his leadership.

The climate is sacred . . . but distant.

Purposeful . . . but lonely.

The unspoken message Samuel may absorb:

I am an answer to prayer.
I am a living sacrifice.
My belonging is tied to my usefulness.

This story speaks tenderly to women
who were raised by mothers who loved God
but could not be emotionally present.

Mothers who were duty-bound,
exhausted,
depressed,
overwhelmed—
doing their best,
yet unable to offer consistent attunement.

You can become steady and responsible while still carrying a
quiet ache for comfort.

God does not shame this ache.
He meets it.

The Canaanite Woman: A Mirror of What Was Missing

This story is different.

Here is a mother who refuses to be silent when her child is
suffering.
She presses past barriers.
She endures dismissal.
She advocates fiercely.

And for women with a mother wound,
this story can awaken grief—
not because of what is present,
but because of what wasn't.

It may stir the question:

What would it have been like . . .
to have someone fight for me like that?

This story does not accuse your mother.
It simply reveals the hunger.

And Jesus does not shame this mother's persistence.
He honors it.

Which tells us something sacred:

God welcomes the longing for a love that shows up,
speaks up,
and refuses to disappear.

The Climate of Mothering and the Messages It Seeds

Mother wounds are less about one event and more about an
emotional atmosphere.

Here are a few common climates—
not to label, but to gently name.

The Fog of Depression

A mother physically present, emotionally absent.

The child learns:

My joy is too much.
My needs overwhelm her.
I must be small to keep the peace.

The Prisoner of Resentment

Care is given,
but without delight.

The child learns:

My existence is a burden.
I must earn my place.

The Daughter Who Became the Mother

The roles reverse.

The child learns:

My needs come second.
Love means being strong for others.

When the Mother Wound Shapes the God-Image

Here is where the wound often goes deepest:

The climate of our first attachments
can become the subconscious blueprint
for how we experience God.

If love was scarce → God feels withholding.
If care was conditional → grace feels risky.
If invisibility felt safer → God's gaze feels exposing,
not comforting.

This is not spiritual failure.
It is attachment logic.

And God does not come to silence your story with slogans.
He comes to re-parent the places where love went missing.
So we don't come swinging blame—not at ourselves, and not at
her.

We do this with mercy.
We look with compassion at **the little girl inside you . . .**
and sometimes,
with compassion at **your mother**, too—
because she was often mothering out of what she was given.

**Compassion does not excuse what was harmful;
it simply tells the truth without hatred.**

Healing begins when we can name what we learned:

I learned my needs were a burden.
I learned love must be earned.

And then, with tenderness,
we begin to let God meet those places
with a love that is non-transactional, steady, abundantly present,
and delighted in our mere being.

We rebuild the internal climate.
We reshape the blueprint.
One honest breath at a time.

The God Who Mothers Us

And this is the turning point.
The same place where the wound shaped your God-image . . .
is also the place where God begins to heal it.

Scripture is not shy about this.
It does not whisper this truth—
it speaks it plainly,
tenderly,
and repeatedly.

God reveals Himself not only as Father,
King,
or Shepherd,
but as the **One who mothers us—**
not in replacement of fatherhood,
but in **fullness** of His love.

His comfort is for daughters, too.

"As a mother comforts her child,
so will I comfort you."
—Isaiah 66:13

"Can a mother forget her nursing child,
or lack of compassion for the child of her womb?
Even if these forget, yet I will not forget you."
—Isaiah 49:15

God does not deny the pain.
He names the unthinkable possibility:

Even mothers can fail.

And then He places His love beyond that limitation.

These verses meet the woman
whose story includes abandonment,
neglect,
emotional distance,
or resentment.

God does not minimize her experience.

He acknowledges that human mothering can fracture—
and then He reveals something staggering:

"How often I wanted to gather your children together,
as a hen gathers her chicks under her wings,
but you were not willing!"
—Matthew 23:37

Jesus chooses maternal imagery at the height of His grief.

A hen does not lead from a distance.
She gathers.

She shelters.
She absorbs danger into her own body.

Under her wings is warmth,
protection,
and safety—
a place to hide until the storm passes.

This is the posture of God toward us.
These are not metaphors of convenience.

They are **revelations of God's heart**—
aspects of His nature that maternal imagery helps us receive.

All true mothering reflects Him.

Which means something profoundly healing:

If God cares for us with a mother's tenderness,
then mothering did not originate in humanity.
It originated in Him.

God offers salvation not only from sin—
but **salvation as new attachment**.
Romans 8:15-16; John 14:16-18

The Holy Spirit—the **Parakletos**—
is the Comforter who lives within us.

The Holy Spirit groans for us when words fail.
The Holy Spirit mothers the places that were missed.
And here is the mercy:

Healing does not require revisiting every memory.

If memories come, we meet them gently—but we do not force them.

We heal as we experience new attachment in the present.

This is how the soul rewires.
This is how the feminine heart is restored.

God does not ask you to relive what broke you—
He invites you to receive what was missing.

And before we turn toward the father wound,
we slow down.

Because this . . . **is holy ground.**

If something feels tender right now,
that is not weakness.

That is **awareness.**
That is **your heart waking up.**

Take a breath.

As you read about God as a nurturing Mother,
what did you feel first—
comfort,
resistance,
longing,
confusion,
or grief?

What kind of nurture do you sense you missed or received
inconsistently?

What sentence has your soul longed to hear?
Write it down. Let it breathe.

What would it feel like to receive comfort without needing to
explain yourself?

Where do you feel your body soften—
even slightly—
as you imagine being gathered under His wings?

Nothing is wrong with you for needing comfort.

Need is not weakness—
it is design.

And God does not shame what He Himself created.

A Prayer of Receiving (if you can pray this)

> God,
> I come to You without fixing,
> without explaining,
> without trying to get it right.
>
> I bring You the place in me
> that learned to ask,
> *Will I be cared for?*
>
> The place that wondered
> if my needs were too much,
> if my presence was a burden,
> if love would stay.
>
> I don't come with answers.
> I come with openness.
>
> Would You meet me here—
> not as a taskmaster,
> not as a distant authority,
> but as the One who comforts?
>
> Would You gather the parts of me
> that learned to be quiet,
> self-sufficient,
> or invisible to survive?
>
> Would You speak the words
> my soul longed to hear—
> the ones I didn't have language for
> when I needed them most?

Holy Spirit, Comforter,
I open myself to receive
the nurturing that was missed,
the safety that was inconsistent,
the tenderness my body still remembers needing.

Teach my nervous system
what it feels like to be held
without earning,
to be seen without performing,
to be loved without conditions.

I don't need You to erase my story.
I need You to meet me inside it.

Mother my soul today.
Stay with me.
Teach me how to rest in Your presence
and trust that I will have enough.
Amen.

When you are ready,
we will gently turn toward the second pillar of the soul . . .
the place where strength,
affirmation,
protection,
and calling were meant to form.

But for now:

rest.
God is already here.

Stay here as long as you need.
Nothing else is required of you right now.

We don't **rush** from **mothering** into meaning.
We **rest** here first.

As this place of belonging begins to soften,
another ache often rises—
the ache to be seen, affirmed,
and protected as we step into the world.

This is where the father wound lives.
And it deserves the same tenderness.

Chapter 7

THE FATHER WOUND: WILL I BE PROTECTED?

Where our need for protection and blessing was formed—and where God meets it.

If the mother wound asks,
Will I be cared for?
the father wound asks something different:

Will I be protected?
Am I seen?

Do I have what it takes?
Is there someone strong enough to stand with me in the world?

This is not a louder wound.
But it is often a quieter one—
one that hides in plain sight.

Many women do not name it as grief or pain at all.

Sometimes it looks like competence—
independence—
grit.

Self-reliance.
The ability to carry weight without asking for help.

Many women learned to be strong not because they wanted to
be, but because they had to be.
And sometimes . . .
strength became the safest place to hide.

Beneath the capability,
beneath the resilience,
there can live an ache the soul learned to carry early:

I have to figure this out on my own.
I can't depend on anyone.
I must earn my place here.

This chapter is not about blaming your father.
It is about naming what your nervous system learned—
and allowing that learning to be met with compassion.

How the Father Wound Forms

The father wound does not take only one shape.

It can come through **absence**—
a father who was physically gone or emotionally unavailable.

It can come through **inconsistency**—
warm one moment, withdrawn the next, unpredictable in tone
or presence.

It can come through **harshness**—
criticism outweighing affection, expectations eclipsing delight.

It can even come through **goodness without attunement—**
a father who provided materially but never learned how to see
the heart of his daughter.

And while some wounds leave a void,
the wound of silence leaves an echo.

It is not that the father was entirely gone—
it is that his essential voice was missing.

The silence where your name should have been spoken with
pride.
The empty space at the dinner table where curiosity about your
day should have lived.
The vacant chair at the recital.
The unmade eye contact after the game.
The newspaper held up like a wall.

He was present—
yet he withheld the most crucial element of his presence:

his engaged,
interested,
affirming voice.

This silence is not neutral.

To a child's soul,
it speaks volumes.

It translates as:

You are not interesting enough to capture my attention.
Your achievements are not worthy of my celebration.
Your inner world is not a place I care to explore.
You exist on the periphery of my real life.

In this silence,
a daughter learns to shout without making a sound.

She may become a high achiever,
screaming for notice through accomplishment.

Or she may become a people-pleasing shadow,
shaping herself into whatever form she believes might finally
earn approval.

She learns that love is not a given,
but something earned through performance.

Her worth becomes a question mark,
waiting for an answer that never comes.

The words never spoken.
The protection never felt.
The blessing never given.

And none of this means something was wrong with you.

This is where grit was forged—
the strength you built when blessing was scarce.
And this is where grace will meet you—
not with pressure, but with presence, so you can come home.

How This Wound Shapes a Woman's Strength

This wound quietly shapes how a woman learns to stand in the world.

It influences:

how she relates to authority,
how she hears God's voice,
how she trusts leadership—or resists it,
how she measures her worth,
and how she understands strength.

And often,
without realizing it,
she becomes her own father.

She learns to push herself forward.
To self-correct.
To motivate through pressure.
To perform for approval—or reject it altogether.

She becomes capable.
Driven.
Resilient.

But resilience born from absence always comes at a cost.

Because what the father was meant to give
was not pressure—but **presence.**
Not perfection—but **protection.**
Not performance-based love—but **spoken blessing**.

And just as the mother wound shapes our sense of safety,
the father wound often shapes how we imagine authority itself.

We project earthly silence onto the heavenly realm.
We assume God is distant, disinterested, and withholding.
We believe our prayers vanish into a cosmic void, unheard.

We feel we must perform spiritual gymnastics—
praying longer, serving more, believing harder—
to finally earn a flicker of His attention.

This is not spiritual failure.
It is survival logic—attachment logic—
the nervous system doing what it had to do to survive.

What a Father's Voice Was Meant to Sound Like

Not primarily correction.
Not first instruction.
Not mere authority.

Blessing.

Scripture gives us a moment where fathering is revealed without distortion.

Before Jesus heals anyone,
before He teaches,
before He proves His strength,
He steps into the water—
and the Father speaks.

> "And a voice from heaven said,
> *'This is my beloved Son,*
> *with whom I am well-pleased.'"*
> —Matthew 3:17

Nothing is required of Him in that moment.
No achievement.
No demonstration.
No earning.

The blessing comes before work.
This is grace—blessing before work.
And it heals the grit you learned to carry alone.

This is not a small theological detail.
It is a relational revelation.

It shows us what a father's voice was always meant to do:

to name,
to delight,
to cover—
not **to evaluate.**

This is the voice many women never heard.
And it is okay to feel the ache of that.

The ache is not disloyalty.
It is honesty.

And honesty is where healing begins.

Naming the Father Wound

Before we move forward, let's pause.

If any of this feels tender,
confusing,
or unexpectedly emotional,
pause here.

Nothing is wrong.

This is simply the soul recognizing familiar ground.

You do not need answers yet.
You do not need clarity.

Simply notice what stirs—
without judgment,
without rushing.

When you think about authority,
protection,
or leadership,
what emotion rises first—
trust, fear, distance, pressure, or longing?

What did you learn about approval growing up?
Was it freely given,
inconsistently offered,
or earned through performance?

When you imagine God's strength,
does it feel comforting . . .
or intimidating?

Where in your life do you feel the need to stay strong so you won't be disappointed again?

Let these questions open space,
not conclusions.

Whatever you notice is enough for today.

The Voice That Was Missing

Earthly fathers were never meant to be the Source—
only the first imprint.

So when the imprint is fractured,
many women don't just lose protection.
They lose the sound of being named.

Not *named* as in labeled—
but named as in blessed.

And when that voice is missing,
the soul compensates.

The gospel does not shame what you learned to do to survive.

It simply offers you something stronger than self-reliance:

a Father who speaks.

Not with pressure.
Not with performance.
With presence.

If you've never known that kind of fathering,
it may feel almost too good to trust.
So we won't rush.

We will simply make room for a new possibility:

that the silence you grew up with
does not get the final word.

What the Father Was Meant to Give

Before we go any further, it helps to name this plainly—
not to accuse,
but to clarify what the soul was designed to receive.

A father's role in the soul is not dominance.
It is covering.

At its best, fathering communicates:

I see you.
I delight in who you are.
You are safe with me.
You don't have to prove your worth.
I am proud of you—before you do anything at all.

When this blessing is absent or distorted,
a woman may grow strong—
but never settled.

Capable—
but never rested.

Confident in skill—
but unsure of her inherent worth.

And because this wound often forms later than the mother wound,
it can hide behind success, leadership, and achievement.

A woman may not feel broken here.
She may feel accomplished.

Until exhaustion sets in.
Or faith becomes transactional.

Or authority feels unsafe.
Or rest feels undeserved.

This is not failure.
This is the soul revealing
where it learned to survive
instead of being sent.

A Prayer of Blessing

You may want to read this slowly.
Or place your hand over your heart.
Or close your eyes

There is no right way to receive.

God,

I bring You the places in me that learned to survive without
protection.

The places that learned to perform,
to strive,
to stay guarded.

I bring You my ideas about authority, approval, and
strength—
even the ones I don't yet have words for.

If I learned that love had to be earned,
meet me there.

If I learned that affirmation was scarce,
meet me there.

Would You bless me—
not for what I do,
but for who I am?

Speak over me the words my soul has been waiting to hear:

You are mine.
You are seen.
You are already enough.

I delight in you.

Teach me what strong love feels like.
Teach me what safe authority looks like.
Teach me how to rest under Your care.

I receive Your blessing—
not as theory,
but as presence.

Amen.

You are not losing strength.
You are learning how to carry it differently.

And as this settles, something quiet begins to stir—
not urgency,
not demand,
but invitation.

Before a woman can integrate her strength and softness,
before she can understand her design,
she must first know she is not alone.

That is where we turn next.

Not to effort.
Not to fixing.
But to **receiving.**

Receiving does not erase what was missing.

It gently fills what was never given.

We turn now to the God who re-parents the soul.

Chapter 8

LETTING GOD
RE-PARENT THE SOUL

Receiving what was missing.

Before God restores a woman's wholeness,
He restores her wonder.

Before He heals her fractures,
He reminds her how she was formed.

Long before your childhood,
before your heartbreak,
before you learned to protect yourself,
there was a God who knew your name
and formed you with intention.

Your story did not begin with what went wrong.
It began with design.

And healing does not begin with fixing what broke.
It begins with remembering what was true
before the breaking ever came.

Up to this point, we have named the places where care was
inconsistent,
where affirmation was quiet or absent,
where strength had to be formed too early
and softness began to disappear.

We have named the mother wound—
the ache that asked,
Will I be cared for?

We have named the father wound—
the longing that asked,
Will I be protected?
Will I be seen?
Do I have what it takes?

And now, we slow down.

Here, grit can finally exhale—
because grace is holding what you were never meant to carry.

Because the next movement is not effort.
It is not analysis.
It is not trying to heal harder.

It is receiving.

The Limits of Human Parenting

Earthly parents were never meant to be the source—
only the first mirrors.

They were meant to point beyond themselves,
to reflect something greater,
something truer,
something eternal.

And when the mirror is broken—
through absence, limitation, pain, or wounding—
your soul is not meant to remain trapped there.

We are meant to look beyond the mirror
to the Source.

This is not an indictment of your parents.
It is a kindness toward your hunger.

Because what was missing still matters.
And what you needed still deserves to be met.

God does not ask you to pretend your needs were smaller than
they were.

He invites you to bring the exact shape of your hunger—
the ache for presence,
the longing for affirmation,
the desire for protection and strength—
and open it to Him.

You do not need perfection.
You need posture.

And posture begins with this quiet courage:

What if God is different than what I learned?

A God Who Speaks

Healing begins when we dare to believe
that the heart of God is the opposite of wounding silence.

He is not distant.
He is not withholding.
He is not waiting for you to perform correctly
before He draws near.

He is a God who speaks.
He calls you by name.

> "Do not fear, for I have redeemed you;
> I have called you by name;
> you are mine."
> —Isaiah 43:1

He calls you His child.

> "See what great love the Father has given us that we
> should be called God's children—and we are!"
> —1 John 3:1

He calls you His friend.

> "I do not call you servants anymore . . .
> Instead, I have called you friends."
> —John 15:15

His Word is not a monologue.
It is an invitation into relationship.

Healing deepens when we realize that God is not only restoring
what was withheld—
but pursuing what was hidden.

He is not standing at a distance issuing instruction.
He is drawing near, attentive to the movement of your heart.

Scripture becomes more than truth to understand;
it becomes a place of encounter.
Prayer becomes more than words spoken;
it becomes shared presence.

God does not rush the soul He loves.
He woos it back into trust.
He does not force Himself where the soul is still learning to trust.

He speaks in ways that awaken wonder,
not fear—
desire, not duty.

This is not a romance of emotion,
but of communion:

a sacred nearness where the soul learns again that it is wanted,
delighted in,
and safe to respond.

Which means something important for healing:

We open Scripture not as a textbook,
but as a love letter.

We come to prayer not to perform,
but to wait.

Not expecting the old silence—
but listening for the gentle voice of the Spirit who says:

You are my child.
I see you.
I am well pleased with you in Christ.

The Blessing That Comes Before Performance

Here is where the gospel becomes profoundly personal.
God does not scold you for what you didn't receive.
He supplies it.

Scripture does not present God as a distant authority,
but as a Father who lavishes love.

Lavishing is not restraining.
It is generous.
Unembarrassed.
Overflowing.

At Jesus's baptism—
before a single miracle,
before any teaching,
before any proof of strength—
the Father speaks:

> "This is my beloved Son,
> in whom I am well pleased."
> —Matthew 3:17

Nothing is required of Jesus in that moment.
No achievement.
No demonstration.
No earning.

The **blessing** comes before the work.
This is not a theological detail.
It is a relational revelation.

It shows us what a father's voice was always meant to do:

to name,
to delight,
to cover—
not to evaluate.

If you never heard this kind of voice spoken over you,
it is okay to feel the ache of that.

The ache is not disloyalty.
It is honesty.

And honesty is holy ground.

Re-Parenting the Heart

God does not merely forgive your sins.

He restores what was meant to be formed in love.
He becomes the strong presence who stands behind you.

The voice that affirms instead of evaluates.
The authority that protects instead of threatens.

Where earthly fathering fell short,
God does not shame the gap.
He fills it.

Healing here is not excavation.
It is welcome.

It begins with letting yourself be named—
not by your achievements,
not by your resilience,
not by how much you've survived—
but by your belonging.

You are not self-made.
You are claimed.

You are not alone in the world.
You are held.

And as the mother-love of God teaches your soul to rest,
the father-love of God teaches your soul to rise—
not in striving,
but in security.

This is how the feminine soul is restored.

Not by effort.
By receiving.

You might whisper, simply:

God, will You meet me here?
God, will You sit with me in this?
That is enough.

A Prayer of Receiving

You may want to read this slowly.
Or place your hand over your heart.
Or close your eyes.

There is no right way to receive.

God,

I come to You without fixing,
without explaining,
without trying to get it right.

I bring You the places in me
that learned to survive too early.
The places that learned to perform,
to strive,
to stay guarded.

I bring You my ideas about authority,
about love,
about strength—
even the ones I don't yet have words for.

If I learned that love had to be earned,
meet me there.

If I learned that affirmation was scarce,
meet me there.

If I learned to expect silence or disappointment,
meet me there.

Would You bless me—
not for what I do,
but for who I am?

Speak over me the words
my soul has been waiting to hear:

You are mine.
You are seen.
You are already enough.

I delight in you.
You do not have to prove yourself to be loved.

Teach me what strong love feels like.
Teach me what safe authority looks like.
Teach me how to rest under Your care.

I receive Your love—
not as theory,
but as presence.

Stay with me.
Teach me how to rest in it.

Amen.

What Comes Next

You are not losing strength.
You are learning how to carry it differently.

And as this settles,
something quiet begins to stir—
not urgency,
not demand,
but invitation.

Before a woman can integrate her strength and her softness,
before she can understand her calling,
before she can live from her design,
she must first know she is not alone.

That she is held.
That she is covered.
That she is safe enough to become.

And now—
from this place of belonging—
we are ready to return to the beginning.

To how you were formed.
To why you were created as you were.

We turn now
to the rib.

PART IV

IDENTITY RESTORED

Now identity can
be received, not
performed.

Chapter 9

THE RIB:
HER BLUEPRINT OF IDENTITY

The sacred architecture of feminine belonging.

Before woman ever drew her first breath,
God built her from the bone that shields the lungs—
the place where breath lives.

As if even her origin whispered
what she was always meant to carry:

strength, purpose, and sacred identity.

You will guard life.
You will breathe purpose.
You will stand close to the heart.

She was not formed to be smaller—
she was built to be essential.

In the rib, God hid a revelation—
not an afterthought, but a blueprint,

that woman's design was always meant
to shield, to breathe, to restore,
and **to stand beside** in holy strength.

There is a part of your story that began long before you were born.

A quiet story.
A holy story.
A story about a woman's origin . . .
and her purpose.

Long before your childhood,
long before your heartbreak,
long before the fractures and the surviving
and the remembering . . .
your story began in a garden.

It began with a God who builds with intention,
who designs with poetry,
who reveals identity through the materials He chooses.

And when it came time to create woman—
the crescendo of creation,
the final note in His symphony,
the image-bearer who would embody connection, beauty,
softness, and holy strength—
He did not reach for dust.

He reached for a **rib.**
He reached toward the man's side.
Toward something living.
Something already carrying breath.
Something already close to the beating of a heart.
A **rib.**

Some truths don't whisper.
They hum beneath the surface of every woman's life,
waiting to be remembered.

This is one of them:

You were *built*.
Not merely made.
Built.

Crafted with intention.
Fashioned with artistry.
Constructed by the God who never wastes detail or design.

Before we talk about your wounds,
your survival,
your longing,
your radiance—
we must go back to the beginning,
to the moment God dreamed woman into existence.

Because a woman cannot heal
until she remembers who she was before the fracture.

And God left the clues
in the place He chose to build her from.

You were not merely made—
you were **built with intention, beauty, and holy strength**—
a living sanctuary,
fashioned from the rib, closest to the heart of God.

Why the Rib?
It was God's most intentional choice.

Scripture says:

> "So the Lord God caused a deep sleep to come over the man . . .
> He took one of his ribs . . .
> Then the Lord made the rib he had taken from the man
> into a woman . . ."
> —Genesis 2:21–22

The Hebrew text doesn't say God simply "made" woman.
It uses a word rich with meaning: ***banah***[1].

Banah means:

to build,
to establish,
to adorn,
to architect with intention and beauty.

Not simply *made*.
Not simply *formed*.

But **built**—
the word used for temples, altars, palaces, and cities.

God *built* woman.

A sanctuary.
A masterpiece.

The crescendo of creation.

The final brushstroke of Genesis.

And He built her from the rib.

But rib in Hebrew is richer than English allows.

The word is ***tzelah***[2], meaning:

rib,
side,
and structural beam,
the protected,
holy place,
the place of closeness,
equality,
and communion.

The Hebrew word **tzelah** appears about forty-one times in the
Hebrew Scriptures.

Forty-one times.

And only once—
only here in the garden—
do we translate it *rib*.

Every other time, **tzelah** becomes the language of sanctuary:

the sides of the Tabernacle where glory rested,
the beams of the Temple,
the framing of the Ark.

As if the Bible itself is giving us a theology of woman
before we even know we need one.

As if to say:

She is not merely flesh.
She is sacred architecture.
God built her the way He builds places where He abides.

Woman is a holy structure.

A living sanctuary.
A bearer of the presence of God into human relationship.

The apostle Paul, reflecting on this ancient story,
saw something else hidden in the rib—
something about love,
sacrifice,
and the birthing of new life:

> "For no one ever hates his own flesh,
> but provides and cares for it,
> just as Christ does the church—
> since we are members of his body."
> —Ephesians 5:29–30.

From the side of Adam came his bride;
from the side of Christ, pierced on the cross, came the church.

The rib, it seems,
has always been the place from which God brings forth life.

Scripture doesn't hurry past this detail.
It lingers.
And in the original Hebrew, it leaves us clues.

And when God named what He had built,
He called her ***ezer kenegdo***[3]—
a phrase so powerful that throughout Scripture,
the word ***ezer*** (help) appears 21 times in the Old Testament,
and most often, it refers to God Himself.

She was not built to be less.
She was built to be essential.
A strength equal to.
A help like the One who alone can save.

This word, ***tzelah***, will keep returning,
because Scripture itself keeps returning to it when God speaks
about sacred dwelling and nearness.

This is grit and grace in the same architecture—
protection and nearness.

God could have chosen any bone.
He chose the one that protects what is most essential to life.
Everything God builds in Scripture,
He whispers again in creation.

The rib becomes a living metaphor,
revealing its meaning layer by layer through the body itself.

And nowhere is that whisper louder
than in the rib.

And what does it whisper?
The rib protects the heart.

The Rib Protects the Heart

The heart—
the seat of emotion, connection, and love—
is the first thing the rib guards.

A woman guards what is tender—
not by force,
but by design.

She was formed to shelter what is sacred.

The Rib Protects the Lungs – The Breath of Life

The lungs are where breath becomes life,
where the Spirit moves,
where inhaling becomes communion.

Women carry breath—
spiritually and relationally.

They breathe life into:

rooms,
conversations,
children,
families,
marriages,
communities,
generations.

Her presence expands a room
the way lungs expand beneath the shelter of ribs.

The Science of the Rib: God Hidden in Biology

The more closely we look, the more the rib keeps telling the
same story—
restoration,
resilience,
and return.

Many people don't know this:

under certain conditions,
ribs can regenerate[4].

Did you catch that?
If a rib is removed but its covering—
the periosteum—
remains,
the rib **grows back.**

This regenerative power is so remarkable
that surgeons rely on it.

The rib is one of the few bones in the body
with this capacity for complete restoration—
as if the bone itself were designed
to preach a sermon on return.

This is not an accident.
This is not random biology.

It is God preaching through anatomy.

Just like a woman—
What was taken from you can be restored.
What broke can regrow.
What you lost is not lost forever.

A woman was built from the bone
that knows how to return to itself.

Her story will return.
Her radiance will regrow.
Her heart will be rebuilt.
Her breath will expand again.

No wonder God chose the rib.

It is the architecture of resurrection.

She breaks . . . and builds again.
She is wounded . . . and rises again.
She is stretched . . . and returns stronger.

Ribs Form a Curved Shield—Not a Cage

They do not imprison.
They shelter.
They curve with both strength and softness—
holding space around what is vulnerable.

The shape is intentional:

Strength that bends,
not strength that breaks.

Which leads to the next revelation . . .

The Rib Protects By Flexibility, Not Rigidity

Ribs are strong—
but their strength is not stiffness.

They expand.
They contract.
They bend with every breath.

A rigid rib would shatter.
A flexible rib protects.

A woman's strength mirrors this.

She protects through:

adaptability,
emotional attunement,
resilience,
intuitive responsiveness.

Her strength moves.
Her strength gives.
Her strength creates space for others to breathe.

She was never meant to be rigid—
She was designed to be responsive.

The Rib Holds the Body Together—Structurally

The ribcage is not only protection;
It is architecture.

It anchors:

the muscles of breath,
the muscles of posture,
the core that stabilizes the whole body,
even the muscles required for speaking.

Without ribs:

the body collapses,
the breath shortens,
the voice weakens.

God hid a message here:

Woman was designed to support what gives the body
its strength, its stability,
and its voice.

No wonder the enemy targets a woman's voice—
it's structural.

Ribs Stand at the Side—Not Above or Beneath

Scripture returns to this word again—
tzelah,
the sacred place beside—
because God keeps returning to the theme of nearness.

The same word used for the side of the Ark and the Temple is
the word He chose for woman:

not beneath,
not above,
but beside—
equal,
aligned,
essential.

The Rib and Covenant: A Hidden Biblical Pattern

Scripture seems to be whispering a pattern.

Consider:

Eve from Adam's side.
Blood and water flowing from Jesus's side.

The Ark's ***tzelah***—the place where God's presence dwelled.

Could it be that God builds covenants from the side—
from vulnerability,
from nearness,
from shared breath and shared life?

Woman is a covenant bearer
because she was taken from the place
where covenant lives.

Science and Scripture Say the Same Thing

Woman is:

protective but not imprisoning
soft but unbreakable
flexible but foundational
responsive yet strong
a restorer by design
a sanctuary in motion
a bearer of breath, voice, and life.

Isn't it beautiful how science echoes what Scripture has been saying all along?

Woman is a living sanctuary.

A masterpiece of divine architecture.
Built with intention,
detail, symmetry,
and sacred strength . . .
set-apart for Jesus.

God's Careful Artistry: Built, Not Formed

Now we return to the word that has been carrying us all along.

God formed Adam from the dust.
But He **built** woman from a living, protecting bone.

He did not make her quickly.
He crafted her.

The Hebrew word **banah** carries imagery of:

adorning,
establishing,
architecting with intention,
weaving beauty into structure.

You were not created as an afterthought,
an accessory,
or a solution to loneliness.

You were created as:

a protector of what is sacred,
a bearer of life,
a guardian of hearts,
a companion of breath,
a reflection of strength and tenderness woven together.

This is why the enemy attacks you.
Not because you are weak—
but because you are ***essential.***

When the protector is confused,
the whole house trembles.

When the woman who guards breath is distorted,
the whole family gasps for air.

When the radiance of the one who shelters hearts is dimmed,
generations feel exposed.

But God's blueprint for you
is louder than the enemy's lie.

A Moment from My Own Life

There was a night—
years after my own breaking—
when one of my children came into my room,
heart hurting in a way I didn't know how to fix.

I sat beside her,
not above, not in front—
beside.

As she cried,
I placed my hand over her heart,
the same place God protected with ribs,
and I whispered a prayer.

Not to be her savior.
Not to fix.
But simply to cover
in the way God designed woman to cover.

And in that quiet moment, I realized:

This is what the rib looks like in real life.

Protecting the sacred.
Guarding the vulnerable.
Breathing safety into fear.

Not through striving.
Not through perfection.
But through **presence.**

Women protect not with armor—
but with proximity.

> "I will put breath in you,
> and you will live."
> —Ezekiel 37:5

As God spoke to dry bones:

> *"I will put breath in you,
> and you will live."*

God built woman from the bone that guards breath,
a living reminder that she is invited to guard
what makes life worth living.

You may want to sit with these slowly.

Where have you forgotten
that you were *built*—
not merely made?

What would it change to reclaim **banah**
as your origin story?

What sacred things has God asked you to protect—
your heart, your children,
your breath, your boundaries,
your voice?

Where have you acted like a cage instead of a shelter—
and where have you allowed others to cage you
instead of honoring your God-given design
to stand side by side?

What part of your radiance has been buried beneath
responsibility,
and what might it feel like
to let God rebuild that place within you?

A Blessing for Your Design

Beloved,
may you remember that you were **built**—
not hastily formed,
but sacredly fashioned.

May the God who chose the rib
remind you of your strength,
your softness,
your holy purpose
to guard what is sacred
and breathe life into what has grown faint.

May you feel His breath
restoring your own,
and may you rise again
as the sanctuary He designed—
curved in compassion,
rooted in strength,
and radiant in the truth
that you were created
from the side of love itself.

As you begin to remember the beauty of your design—
the protection in your presence,
the strength in your softness,
the sanctuary woven into your very bones—
something subtle but important shifts.

Knowing who you were created to be
is not the same as learning how to live from that place.

Design reveals identity;
embodiment teaches us how to dwell inside it.

Design is revelation.
Embodiment is practice.

And this is where many women quietly stumble—
not because they are unwilling,
but because they were never given permission
to be human while healing.

So before radiance is carried outward,
before strength is expressed in the world,
there is a holy pause.

A place where identity moves out of theory
and into the body.

Where truth is not performed
but felt.

Where healing is not demanded
but received.

This is where healing becomes embodied.

Where breath returns.
Where needs are named.
Where the woman God designed
begins to live gently inside her own skin again.

And from that gentle place,
from that holy pause,
you are invited not to strive,
but to receive once more.

A Blessing for the Journey Inward

May you rest in Jesus—
not earning, but receiving.
May you remember your divine design—
not as a standard to achieve,
but as a truth to inhabit.
May you sit in gentle presence
with yourself and with others,
letting identity move from your mind into your bones.

And may you respond—
not from striving,
but from the quiet abundance of a life stewarded,
offering to the world
what He has already placed in you.

We step now onto holy ground—not to strive,
but to listen.

SACRED GROUND:
MEETING YOURSELF HONESTLY

When the counseling room becomes holy ground.

There comes a moment in every woman's healing
when the ground beneath her shifts—
not because her circumstances change,
but because she finally sees herself clearly.

And that clarity is not condemnation.
It is **consecration.**

For the woman built from the rib,
honesty is not humiliation.

It is ***holiness***.

This is the chapter where she stops performing.
Stops hiding.
Stops explaining herself away.
Stops apologizing for being human.

And begins meeting the woman God has always seen clearly.

This is sacred ground.

> "The angel of the LORD found her by a spring in the
> wilderness . . .
> Then she called the LORD who spoke to her:
> 'You are El-Roi.
> In this place,
> have I actually seen the one who sees me?'"
> —Genesis 16:7–13

Known— John 4

Jesus tells the truth and stays near.

> "'Go call your husband', Jesus told her,
> 'and come back here' . . .
> You're right in saying, 'I don't have a husband.
> For you've had five husbands . . .'"
> —John 4:16–18

Don't miss this.

He names her story without flinching—
and then something even more stunning happens:

she doesn't fold in shame.

She leaves her water jar, runs back into town, and says out loud,
Come, see a man who told me everything I ever did.

Not whispered.
Not hidden.
Not managed.

She returns to people who already know her story—
and she goes anyway.

Because when the One who sees you stays near,
shame loses its grip.

Not condemned— John 8

Mercy meets you in the exposed place.

> "Neither do I condemn you", said Jesus.
> "Go, and from now on do not sin anymore."
> —John 8:11

He does not cover you with denial.
He covers you with mercy.
And that is how shame loses its name.

This is the place where identity begins to rebuild,
not from trauma,
but from truth.

Identity Embodied: Who She Is in Real Life

As the woman steps onto this sacred ground, she realizes:

Her wounds weren't random—
they were targeted.

Against her identity.
Against her design.
Against her enoughness.

Every behavior she wrestled with
began with a belief she absorbed in pain.

This is why Scripture says:

> "Do not be conformed to this age,
> but be transformed by the renewing of your mind."
> —Romans 12:2

We do not live from reality.
We behave from what we believe is true.

Which means:

to restore a woman,
God must restore her beliefs.

The Lies She Learned to Live From

Here we speak gently but clearly:

I am too much.
I am not enough.
My needs don't matter.
I must carry everything.
I can't disappoint anyone.
My voice causes problems.
If I rest, everything will fall apart.
If I soften, I'll get hurt.
I have to earn love.

These are not personality traits.
They are false gospels.

They are belief systems forged in pain.

And every false belief must be met—
not with willpower,
but with truth.

Grit tells the truth; grace holds you while you do.

Strength Built on Fear vs. Strength Built on Truth

There is a kind of strength women wear
that looks holy,
sounds noble,
and is praised by everyone around her . . .
but is secretly fueled by fear.

Fear-based strength says:

If I don't hold everything together, it will fall apart.
If I have needs, I will become a burden.
If I stop being strong, someone will be disappointed in me.
If I let go, I will lose control.
If I soften, I will be hurt again.

Fear-based strength is loud,
rigid,
performative,
and exhausting.

Fear-based strength lives in the body:

the jaw,
the shoulders,
the calendar,
the silence,
the over-functioning,
the perfectionism.

It builds a fortress,
but not a home.
It protects you from pain—
but also from connection.

This strength is not sin.
It is survival.

But there is another strength:

Holy strength.
Rib strength.
The strength you were built with.

Strength that flows from being held,
not from holding everything.

Truth-based strength sounds like:

God is with me—therefore I can rest.
I do not have to be everything for everyone.
I am allowed to need.
I can soften without shattering.
I can stand without striving.
I can breathe because God holds what I cannot.

This is the strength Eve knew
before fear entered the world—
strength that flows from being held,
not from holding everything.

Truth-based strength is:

peaceful,
flexible,
rooted,
open,
compassionate,
stable.

It is less like armor
and more like breath.

This is the strength Scripture speaks of:

> "You will be delivered by returning and resting:
> your strength will lie in quiet confidence."
> —Isaiah 30:15

"The joy of the Lord is your strength."
—Nehemiah 8:10

"My grace is sufficient for you,
for my power is perfected in weakness."
—2 Corinthians 12:9

Truth-based strength is not something you earn.
It rises in you when fear no longer gets the final say.

One strength defends your life.
The other restores it.

The Girl Who Believed She Had to Earn Love

She was nineteen—
a sophomore—
sitting cross-legged on the floor of my office because she said
couches made her feel *too big*.

Her name is Emmie.
And the way she folded her hands in her lap,
as if trying to make herself smaller,
is something I will never forget.

She said softly,
I know people love me . . .
I just feel like I have to earn it every day.

When I asked her where she learned that,
she stared toward the corner of the room—
the place people look when remembering something
they've tried to outrun.

Probably when I was eight, she whispered.
My dad got so happy when I got things right . . .

and so cold when I didn't.
It just felt easier to be perfect than to disappoint him.

Then came the sentence that broke something open inside me:

I don't want to be loved because I perform.
But I don't know who I am without performing.

She didn't know it,
but she had just spoken the oldest lie women carry:

If I stop striving, love will leave.

When I told her she didn't have to earn
what God already called *hers*,
her eyes filled—not with sorrow,
but with the shock of being told something
she always suspected
but never dared to believe:

You were loved before you ever did anything right.

That moment became holy ground—
a remembering,
a returning,
a girl meeting herself
without the weight of perfection.

The Girl Who Thought She Was *Too Much*

Susie walked into the coffee shop laughing—
loud, bright, beautiful laughter
that filled the room before she even sat down.

But as soon as we began talking,
her shoulders folded inward
like wings she wasn't sure she was allowed to open.

I've been told my whole life that I'm a lot, she said.
Too emotional.
Too expressive.
Too intense.
Too passionate.
Too . . . everything.

She tried to laugh,
but her voice cracked right in the middle.

I think people like pieces of me . . .
just not the whole me.

And then she whispered the sentence
that so many women bury inside themselves:

I've been trying to shrink myself
so I don't overwhelm people.

I asked her what it felt like,
living as a small version of a big soul.

She stared at the floor for a long moment
and finally said:

It feels like I disappear a little bit every year.

Her *too much* was never chaos.
It was radiance.
It was passion.
It was the breath of God moving freely inside her.

But somewhere along the way,
someone told her that her light was inconvenient,
and she believed them.

When I told her,
You were never too much—
you were just too bright for people who had forgotten their own light,

she cried like someone had opened a window
in a room she'd been locked in.

The Mother Who Forgot She Was Allowed to Have a Heart

She came into my office on a Thursday morning—
hair in a messy bun,
leggings dusty from the playground,
a diaper bag on one shoulder
and exhaustion on the other.

Before she even sat down, she exhaled the sentence
so many mothers feel
but rarely say:

I don't know who I am anymore.

Her eyes filled as she tried to smile through it.
I love my kids.
I wouldn't trade being their mom for anything.
But somewhere along the way . . .
I think I misplaced myself.

She told me how she woke up every day already behind,
giving, giving, giving,
until there was nothing left
but the noise inside her own mind.

My kids get all my patience.
My husband gets what's left.
God gets whatever scraps I have at night.
And I get . . . Nothing.

When I gently asked her
when she first learned that her needs were optional,
she pressed her fingers to her eyelids
like she was steadying her soul.

When my mom said she was fine
even when she clearly wasn't.

She swallowed hard.
I thought that's what strong women do.

Then came the confession mothers carry silently:

I feel guilty wanting anything for myself.

She wasn't selfish.
She wasn't neglectful.
She wasn't broken.

She was a rib
forced to hold an entire body upright
while her own breath kept getting shorter.

I asked her,
What do you miss about yourself?

She didn't answer right away.
Then one tear slid down her cheek as she whispered:

I miss my laugh.
I miss feeling light.
I miss not apologizing for being human.

Holy ground.
A mother remembering she is not only a giver of life
but a carrier of breath.

A rib that protects the sacred—
including her own soul.

So I told her what I now say to you:

You were never meant to disappear
inside the people you love.
Your heart matters too.

And for the first time in years,
she let herself believe it.

Each story ends not with fixing,
but with recognition—
a woman being seen,
a lie being named,
a body finally softening.

That is sacred ground.

This is grace—being seen without shame.

And this is grit—telling the truth without disappearing.

Where Lies Break and Identity Begins

Every woman carries beliefs she never consciously chose.
Beliefs shaped by wounds.
Beliefs shaped by silence.
Beliefs shaped by years of trying to be *okay* when she was
unraveling inside.

But the gospel is not behavior modification.
It is identity restoration.

And identity is not rewritten by striving—
it is rewritten by truth.

Truth does not shout; **it settles.**

And when truth is believed, something begins to shift:

shoulders soften
her voice steadies
breath deepens
striving loosens
boundaries strengthen

her tenderness returns
radiance rises,

Because truth creates safety.
And safety creates transformation.

Scripture says:

> "Then you will know the truth,
> and the truth will set you free."
> —John 8:32

Freedom does not begin with trying harder.
It begins with letting God speak truer words
than the ones pain spoke first.

Disrupting the Lies with Truth

Below is a lie disrupted by Scripture,
each false belief undone by the voice of God.

> **Lie:** *I am too much.*
> **Truth:** "You are fearfully and wonderfully made."
> —Psalm 139:14

God never calls what He crafted *too much.*
Your fullness is intentional.

> **Lie:** *I am not enough.*
> **Truth:** "My grace is sufficient for you."
> —2 Corinthians 12:9

You are not meant to be everything—
you are meant to be held by the One who is.

Lie: *My needs don't matter.*
Truth: "Cast all your cares on Him,
for He cares for you."
—1 Peter 5:7

Needs are not weakness.
They are invitations to connection.

Lie: *I must carry everything alone.*
Truth: "The Lord is my strength and my shield;
my heart trusts in him, and I am helped."
—Psalm 28:7

You were never meant to be the whole shield.
You were designed to reflect the One who is.

Lie: *If I rest, everything will fall apart.*
Truth: "You will be delivered by returning and resting;
your strength will lie in quiet confidence."
—Isaiah 30:15

Rest is not a luxury—
it is obedience.

Lie: *If I soften, I will get hurt again.*
Truth: "He will cover you with His feathers,
and under His wings you will find refuge."
—Psalm 91:4

Softness in God's presence is safety, not danger.

Lie: *My voice causes problems.*
Truth: "She speaks with wisdom,
and loving instruction is on her tongue."
—Proverbs 31:26

Your voice is not a disruption—
it is design.

Lie: *I have to earn love.*
Truth: "I have loved you with an everlasting love,
therefore, I have continued to extend faithful love
to you."
—Jeremiah 31:3

His love was never based on performance—
and it cannot be undone by imperfection.

You might pause here and ask yourself—without pressure:

What lie has spoken the loudest in my life?
Where did I first learn it?
What truth feels like relief, not demand?

Let these questions rest.
They are not assignments.
They are invitations.

Breath Practice: Returning to Your Body

Inhale: God is with me.
Exhale: I can rest.
Inhale: I am loved.
Exhale: I am enough.

Declaration of Truth for the Woman Remembering Herself

Take a breath
and put a hand over your heart.
Let these words move from your mouth into your bones.

Read them slowly.
Out loud.

Like a woman returning home:

I am not what happened to me.
I am who God designed me to be.

I am not too much.
I am the exact measure God intended.

I am not inadequate.
I am fully equipped, deeply loved, and divinely chosen.

I do not earn love.
I receive love because love Himself lives in me.

My needs are not a burden.
They are invitations for connection.
I do not have to hold everything together.
God holds me—and He holds what I cannot hold.

I release survival.
I choose truth.

I release fear.
I choose trust.

I release striving.
I choose rest.

My voice matters.
My presence matters.
My heart matters.

I am allowed to take up space.
I am allowed to breathe.
I am allowed to be human.

I am not defined by my wounds.
I am defined by the One who heals them.

I reclaim the radiance I buried.
I welcome the strength I silenced.
I honor the softness I hid.

God's image is in me.
His breath is in me.
His design is in me.

I stand in the truth that I am:

Loved.
Seen.
Known.
Held.
Restored.
Becoming whole.
Amen.

Let your body learn what your mind is remembering.
This is not imagination.
This is memory—
a woman remembering who she was
before pain spoke louder than truth.

Before you turn the page, pause.

You are not leaving with a list to fix.
You are leaving with a felt sense of who you are.
And that matters.

When a woman begins to live from identity instead of injury,
something else begins to surface—
not effort,
not striving,
but design.

Gifts God placed within you
before you ever learned to protect yourself.

Not goals to achieve.
Identities to remember.

PART V

BECOMING WHOLE

Healing moves from
insight to embodiment.

Chapter 11

THE FOUR GIFTS
OF THE FEMININE SOUL

Remembering what was always there.

This chapter was not written to be rushed.

You may want to read it slowly.
You may want to linger with one woman's story and skim another.
You may want to come back to these pages again and again—
not because you missed something,
but because something here is meeting you.

There is no finish line in this chapter.
No right pace.
No expectation to resonate with every story.

Some women will feel like mirrors.
Others will feel like companions.
All of them are witnesses.

If you notice emotion rising, pause.
If a sentence feels tender, breathe.
If a story feels familiar,
place a hand over your heart
and let yourself be seen.

This chapter is not asking you to become someone new.
It is inviting you to remember who you already are.

Read it the way you would walk through a garden—
not to check off every path,
but to notice where your attention is drawn.

What you need will meet you.

And when you are ready,
the women here will still be waiting for you.

Before a woman ever learned to survive,
before she learned to shrink, strive, or harden,
God placed gifts inside her.

Not accomplishments.
Not expectations.
Design.

These gifts were not given after healing.
They were present before the wound.

Healing does not create these gifts.
Healing reveals them.

Grace is what reveals what was always there.
Grit is the courage to live from it again.

When God chose the rib,
He chose the place of protection,
breath,

closeness,
and regeneration.

And inside that design,
He hid four sacred gifts
that rise again as identity is restored.

You may see yourself clearly in one woman's story.
You may recognize pieces of yourself in many.

You are not asked to compare.
Only to receive.

These women are not ideals.
They are witnesses.

They stand beside you and whisper:

You come from a long line of women like this.

The Four Gifts of the Feminine Soul

Each gift flows from the rib—
from how woman was formed
and how God continues to restore her.

GIFT ONE — Heart Protection
You Were Built to Guard What Is Sacred

A woman was created from the bone that guards the heart.

Which means:

You were designed to protect what matters most.

Not through hardness, but through discernment.
Not through walls, but through wisdom.
Not through control, but through clarity.

This is why women *feel* what others cannot see.
This is why a woman senses pain,
dishonesty,
danger,
or emotional disconnection
long before anyone else notices.

It is not hypersensitivity.
It is **holy sensitivity—**
the spiritual intelligence woven into your design.

You were built from the rib,
and the rib's first assignment was simple and sacred:

Protect the heart.

When a woman heals,
this protective instinct becomes clear,
steady,
life-giving—
no longer fueled by fear,
but by truth.

Grace steadies her. Grit strengthens her.
Let's look at an example from the Bible.

Deborah – Strength That Breathes Wisdom and Peace

> "A mother in Israel."
> —Judges 5:7

Deborah did not lead Israel with aggression—
she led with presence.

Her leadership flowed from:

steadiness
discernment
spiritual clarity
deep maternal devotion

Scripture says:

> "Villagers in Israel would not fight; they held
> back . . . until I, Deborah, arose, a mother in Israel."
> —Judges 5:7

Deborah reveals that feminine power is not domination—
it is stability wrapped in compassion.

She protected a nation not with a sword,
but with a listening heart
and a courageous voice.

She sensed danger before others saw it.
She stood between fear and her people.
She spoke truth with tenderness and authority.
She shielded a generation with wisdom.

Deborah embodies this truth:

A woman's intuition is not weakness—
it is weaponry.

Heart protection is a spiritual assignment.

It is the feminine gift of:

discernment
attunement
emotional intelligence
sacred bravery

> "Guard your heart,
> for everything you do flows from it."
> —Proverbs 4:23

This is not a command for isolation.
It is a call to stewardship.

To guard the sacredness God placed within you.

And when a woman remembers who she is,
this gift becomes joyfully powerful again.

Deborah modeled this for us.

When a woman remembers who she is,
her protective wisdom rises not from fear—
but from the radiance God placed within her.

Her intuition is not fragility—
it is the Spirit whispering through her design.

GIFT TWO — Breath Bringing
You Were Built to Carry Life Into Weary Places

Ribs expand to make room for breath—
and so does woman.

She makes room for emotions,
dreams,
people,
God's presence.

This gift is written into her body.

Every breath she takes is an act of expansion—
a quiet reminder that she was built to carry life without
collapsing under it.

A woman's presence changes the atmosphere.

Her words revive.
Her prayers shift rooms.
Her tenderness resurrects what fear has smothered.
Her faith becomes oxygen for the weary.

This is not metaphor—
it is design.

Mary — The Capacity to Hold What Is Sacred

> "See, I am the Lord's servant, said Mary.
> May it happen to me according to your word."
> —Luke 1:38

Mary carried Christ Himself—
in her body, in her breath, in her obedience.

Her yes did not come from fear, but from identity.

Before she carried Jesus in her womb,
she carried the breath of surrender in her heart.

Her yes became the doorway
through which God breathed hope into the whole world.

Mary's yes made room for life—
for a fearful fiancé,
for a newborn Savior,
for hope in a darkened nation,
for quiet strengthening of those who would carry the gospel
forward.

She shows us that a woman's consent to God
makes room for miracles.

Her presence—her breath—changes history.

The Feminine Calling to Breathe Life

Women *breathe life* into places that have grown weary, discouraged, or forgotten.

This is why:

When a woman enters a room, the atmosphere shifts.
When she speaks hope, tired hearts lift.
When she prays, battles turn.
When she nurtures, dead things revive.

A woman was built to carry breath.

To expand under pressure.
To release life when others are collapsing.

This is holy breath-bearing—
the ability to nurture,
revive,
and restore the people entrusted to her.

> "Lord God formed the man out of the dust from the ground and breathed the breath of life into his nostrils, and the man became a living being."
> —Genesis 2:7

Women echo that breath as they give life emotionally, spiritually, and relationally.

When a woman remembers who she is,
the next generation breathes differently.

Her breath becomes blessing.
Her presence becomes oxygen.
Her yes becomes legacy.

And when a woman remembers who she is,
this gift becomes radiantly powerful again.

Mary models this for us.

Her breath-bearing was not duty—
it was identity lived out loud.

GIFT THREE — Sacred Connection
You Were Built for Withness, Not Disappearance

When God chose the rib,
He chose the bone of closeness.

Not the head—where one rules.
Not the feet—where one is beneath.

But the side—
the place of equality,
companionship,
closeness,
and shared breath.

Woman was built from the place of *withness*.

This means:

You were designed for relational depth—
not neediness,
but nearness.

You were designed to stand beside,
to walk with,
to be heart-close to the ones entrusted to you.

This is why women hunger for:

emotional intimacy,
meaningful conversation,
shared experience,

connection without performing,
belonging without shrinking,

This hunger is not weakness—
it is wiring.

Sacred wiring.

Connection is the architecture of the feminine soul.

Ruth — Covenant Presence

> "Where you go, I will go . . ."
> —Ruth 1:16

Ruth's story is not loud.

It does not arrive with fanfare.

It unfolds in the ordinary rhythms of grief, loyalty, and brave presence.

And yet—
it becomes one of Scripture's most powerful pictures of feminine connection.

Ruth stayed.
Not out of obligation.
Not out of fear.
But out of covenant love.

She did not disconnect in her pain.
She did not abandon Naomi in despair.

She joined her—
heart to heart,
shoulder to shoulder,
step by step.

Her tenderness became strength.
Her loyalty became redemption's doorway.
Her connection rebuilt a lineage that would lead to:

Boaz
David
Christ Himself

Ruth shows us:

Connection is not weakness—it is covenant strength.

Her presence stitched a broken family back together.
Her devotion restored a future beyond anything she could imagine.

Ruth embodies the gift of sacred connection:

the ability to remain,
to love faithfully,
to bring warmth into cold places
and hope into grieving ones.

What This Reveals About You

A woman feels emotional abandonment with unique depth
because she was built—literally—
for connection.

This is why disconnection wounds.

Why emotional distance feels like suffocation.
Why belonging matters so much.
Your longing for closeness
is not a flaw—
it is a calling.

Woman was created as God's remedy for isolation.

Not as a burden.

As a blessing.

> "Then the Lord God said,
> It is not good for the man to be alone . . ."
> —Genesis 2:18

You were made to be a living sanctuary:

a place where others feel seen,
safe,
understood,
welcomed into warmth.

And when a woman heals,
she no longer disappears in relationships.

She brings her whole self—
and her presence becomes a holy place
where others encounter the tenderness of God.

When a woman remembers who she is, her radiance rises.

She connects without losing herself.
She loves without shrinking.
She stands beside without being consumed.

Her relationships become spaces of redemption,
not depletion.

And when a woman remembers who she is,
this gift becomes joyfully powerful again.

Ruth modeled this for us.

A healed woman becomes a connector,
a restorer,
a builder of legacy

through the quiet courage of staying close
in all the ways that matter.

GIFT FOUR — Regeneration
You Were Built to Rise Again

Science echoes what Scripture whispered first:

the rib can heal—
and under the right conditions, it can even regrow.

It rebuilds itself with the help of its living covering—
a thin protective layer called the periosteum.

In the same way, a woman often rises again
when even a thin covering of hope remains—
even if everything else has been stripped away.

This is not just metaphor.
It is design.

Woman breaks—
and rises.

Woman aches—
and rebuilds.

Woman loses—
and becomes again.

Woman shatters—
and gathers her radiance piece by piece
until she glows again.

This regenerative strength is not learned.
It is inherited.

Hagar — Seen in the Wilderness

> "You are El-Roi . . .
> Have I actually seen the one who sees me?"
> —Genesis 16:13

Hagar's suffering was not chosen.

She was misunderstood,
mistreated, used, and driven into the desert—
twice.

And twice,
God met her there.

Not in a temple.

Not in a sanctuary.

Not in a place of spiritual performance.

God met her in the wilderness—
the place she thought would finish her.

He restored her.
He spoke identity over her.

He blessed her child.

He opened her eyes to a well
in the very place she felt abandoned.

Hagar became the first woman in Scripture to name God—
not because life was easy,
but because God revealed Himself
in the place she felt most unseen.

Don't miss this part.

Hagar was used,
mistreated,
silenced,
and cast into the desert—
pregnant,
alone,
and utterly unseen
by the people who should have protected her.

And yet . . .

It is Hagar—
not Abraham the patriarch,
not Sarah the matriarch,
not Moses the deliverer,
not David the king—
but Hagar,
a marginalized,
oppressed Egyptian servant woman,
who is the first person recorded in Scripture to call Him
El Roi—The God Who Sees Me.

Many in Scripture built altars and named places to remember
what God had done:

The LORD Will Provide— Abraham
The LORD Is My Banner— Moses
The LORD Is Peace— Gideon

But Hagar does something rarer.

She doesn't name a place.
She names the God who met her there—
El Roi—The God Who Sees Me.

This is **holy ground.**

For a woman to name God,
she must have encountered Him not as an idea,

but as a Presence
who meets her in the place
she thought she would die.

Hagar shows us:

God does not only reveal Himself to the powerful.

He reveals Himself to the wounded woman in the wilderness.

Hagar's naming of God is the ultimate act of feminine resilience:

She did not name God from a palace—
she named Him from a desert.

She did not name Him after a victory—
she named Him after abandonment.

She did not name Him when she felt strong—
she named Him when she felt invisible.

Only a woman who knows who she is without titles,
status,
or approval
could speak such revelation:

You are the God who sees me.

Not *us.*

Not *them.*

Not *the chosen.*

Me.

Her identity was not found in her position—
but in God's vision.

And because God saw her,
she was able to see herself again.

Hagar reveals the deepest truth of feminine resilience:

A woman can be:

cast out
unwanted
wounded
forgotten
used
betrayed
and alone . . .
and still rise in identity
the moment she realizes God sees her.

Why this moment matters for your story:

Hagar was not restored through people—
but through **Presence.**

She was not rebuilt through affirmation—
but through **encounter.**

She was not strengthened through circumstance—
but through **being seen**.

This is **regeneration.**
This is **rib strength.**

This is feminine identity restored in the wilderness.

Hagar shows us that true resilience is not self-reliance—
it is being seen by God in the place you thought would break
you.

Because when God sees a woman,
He restores her identity first—
and her story next.

God does not only meet women in holy places.

He meets them in hard places.

And the miracle of Hagar's story
is the same miracle embedded in the rib:

God never lets a woman break
without also rebuilding her.

He begins not with correction,
but with visibility.
I see you.

Hagar is the picture of feminine regeneration:

a woman who rises again
not because she is strong,
but because God restores.

What This Reveals About You

The regenerative nature of womanhood
is not a personality trait.

It is a spiritual inheritance.

The God who made the rib a bone capable of remarkable healing
made woman the carrier of resurrection stories.

Even in your wilderness moments—
the places you thought would undo you—
God was already opening a well.

Even in your breaking moments—
He was already preparing your rebuilding.

Even in your exile moments—
He was already writing legacy.

Resilience is not the force of your will.
It is the resurrection power of God
woven into your design.

When a woman remembers who she is,
her radiance rises.

Not because she never breaks,
but because she never stays broken.

She regenerates.
She rebuilds.
She reclaims her breath.
She returns to the woman God always knew.

> "I will repay for the years the swarming locusts ate."
> —Joel 2:25

> "Strength and honor are her clothing."
> —Proverbs 31:25

> "We are afflicted in every way . . .
> but not crushed."
> —2 Corinthians 4:8

The stories of women in Scripture are not distant biographies—
they are mirrors.

Mirrors that reveal the gifts in you:

heart protection, breath-bearing, sacred connection,
and this:

holy regeneration.

When God breathes through a woman's life,
He is whispering the truth of who you already are:

You were created to rise again.

Women Who Carried These Gifts Before You

The women of Scripture are not ornaments in a biblical story—
they are blueprints.

Living, breathing reflections of the very gifts
God placed inside you.

They show us what feminine radiance looks like
when it rises in real life—
in trauma,
in calling,
in the wilderness,
in ordinary days,
in holy moments.

Their stories do not ask you to compare yourself.

They do not demand imitation.
They simply stand beside you and whisper:

You come from a long line of women like this.

So as you continue turning inward—
as you keep meeting yourself honestly—
let these women gather around you.

Not as ideals.

As witnesses.

As sisters.

Take a breath.

Let your shoulders soften.
Let your heart come forward.

Let's look at four more women in Scripture.

1. Miriam — Breath Bearer Through Worship
The Gift of Breath-Bringing

> "Then the prophet Miriam, Aaron's sister,
> took a tambourine in her hand . . ."
> —Exodus 15:20–21

Israel stood on the other side of the Red Sea—
traumatized,
exhausted,
unsure how to hope again.

It was Miriam who lifted the first song.

Before plans.
Before certainty.
Before strength returned.

Her worship breathed courage into a people learning how to
breathe again.

Miriam teaches us that a woman's breath—
her voice, her presence, her praise—
can steady trembling hearts.

This gift lives in you.

You carry breath into heavy places.
Your presence changes the atmosphere.
Your voice matters, even when it shakes.

Where has your presence brought life into weary places?
Where might God be inviting you to let joy return—
even quietly?

You are allowed to sing again.

2. Esther — Sacred Discernment and Courage
The Gift of Heart Protection

> "Who knows, you have come to your royal position for
> such a time as this."
> —Esther 4:14

Esther did not rush the palace.

She listened.
She waited.
She discerned.

Her courage was not loud—it was precise.

She protected her people not with force,
but with wisdom, timing, and presence.

This gift lives in you.

Your discernment is not weakness.
Your intuition is not fear.
Your caution is not failure.

You were built to protect what is sacred.

Where have you sensed something before others could name it?
Where is God inviting you to trust the wisdom He placed in you?

Breathe.

You do not need to force your strength.

3. Hannah — Sacred Connection Through Prayer
The Gift of Emotional and Spiritual Connection

> "With a broken heart . . .
> I've been pouring out my soul before the Lord."
> —1 Samuel 1:15

Hannah's ache was dismissed by people—
but received by God.

Her tears became prayer.
Her prayer became surrender.
Her surrender became legacy.

Hannah teaches us that longing is not weakness—
it is sacred connection.

This gift lives in you.

Your ache matters.

Your prayers matter.

Your vulnerability opens space for God to move.

What longing have you minimized that God wants to receive?
What might be born if you poured your heart out honestly?

Pause.

God is not uncomfortable with your tears.

4. The Bleeding Woman — Holy Persistence
The Gift of Resilience

> "If I just touch His clothes, I'll be made well."
> —Mark 5:28

For twelve years she suffered—
unseen,
unheard,
pushed aside.

And still,
she reached.

Her resilience was not loud.

It was determined.

It was holy.

Jesus did not rebuke her.
He turned toward her.

This gift lives in you.

Your reaching is faith.
Your persistence is sacred.
Your story does not end where you break.

Where have you kept going despite exhaustion?
What does reaching for Jesus look like for you right now?

Your faith is enough.

This gift lives in you.

You rise again.
You rebuild.
You are seen.

Where has God met you in hard places?
What part of you is being restored right now?

You are not invisible.

Before you move on, pause.

You are not being asked to become all of these women.
You are remembering the parts of yourself that already exist.

These gifts rise slowly.

Gently.

In their time.

A Closing Blessing

Beloved,
you are wise like Deborah,
spacious like Mary,
loyal like Ruth,
seen like Hagar,
breath-bearing like Miriam,
courageous like Esther,
honest like Hannah,
and resilient like the woman who reached for healing.

The same God who met them
meets you now.

Take one more breath.

You are safe here.

And you are becoming whole.

May the God who met each one of them
meet you now—
in your questions,
your longing,
your waiting,
your becoming.

May you feel His gaze upon you
as **El Roi**—*the God who sees you.*

May every gift He placed within you
rise again with clarity, strength, softness, and joy.

And may this chapter be the place
where you return to the truth
you were born from:

You were built—not merely made.
Called—not overlooked.
Seen—not forgotten.
Radiant—not broken.

And this remembering will ripple outward.

The world needs the woman
God crafted in you.

Before we turn the page, pause.

Let what has been named settle gently into your body.
Not as information.
As truth.

You are not leaving this chapter with a list to fix.
You are leaving with a felt sense of who you are.

And that matters.

When Healing Becomes Legacy

When a woman begins to live from identity instead of injury,
something shifts beyond her own healing.

It moves outward.
Quietly.
Naturally.
Inevitably.

Healing does not stop at the edges of a woman's heart.
It flows into every life she touches.

Into the people she loves.
Into the generations that come after her.

Whether you are a mother by birth, adoption,
spiritual influence, mentorship, or presence alone—
your healing reshapes the emotional climate around you.

When a woman breathes differently,
her home breathes differently.

When she learns safety,
her children learn safety.

When she lives from truth,
the next generation receives permission to do the same.

This is not about perfection.

It is about presence.
It is not about getting everything right.
It is about no longer passing on what you were never meant to carry.

So we do not turn next toward blame,
we turn toward impact.

Not to judge how you mothered.

But to honor how healing changes the way love moves through you.
The next chapter is not an evaluation.
It is an invitation.

An invitation to see how restoration becomes inheritance.

How healing becomes legacy.
How the woman you are becoming
creates safer ground for those who come after you.

So take one more breath.

You are not behind.
You are not too late.
You are not disqualified.

You are safe.

You are becoming a woman
who mothers from wholeness instead of wounds.

And that is where we go together, next.

Chapter 12

MOTHERHOOD THROUGH RESTORATION

*When healing reshapes generations
that come after you.*

There is something sacred about the hours before dawn.

I have always been an early riser,
but lately I have found myself waking at 3:00 and 4:00 a.m.—
the house still, the world quiet,
my heart stirred awake by words that refuse to wait for daylight.

I move softly through the dark
and up the stairs,
open my laptop,
and begin writing these pages.

And as I write,
I think of my daughter—
awake at these same hours,
cradling her newborn daughter against her chest,
rocking life in her arms, whispering a tiny soul back into peace.

Two women awake before sunrise:

one feeding a child,
the other feeding a legacy.

Both mothering in different ways.
Both shaping the world of a little girl who will one day grow
into a woman with a story,
a calling,
and a God-written identity of her own.

And it struck me one morning that motherhood is not limited
to biology. It is not confined to cribs or diaper bags or sleepy
feedings in the dark.

Motherhood is influence.

Motherhood is presence.

Motherhood is the way a woman nurtures the world around
her—
through her healing,
her voice,
her radiance,
her resilience.

Every woman mothers someone or something:
a child,
a classroom,
a community,
a friend,
a calling,
a broken heart,
a younger version of herself who still needs gentleness to grow.

So as we step into this chapter, hear this clearly:

This is for every woman.

And before we go any further, I want to name something tender—
because I can feel it in so many women as they read a chapter
like this.

You may be carrying guilt.
The kind that whispers,
I didn't do it right.

The kind that replays seasons you can't redo.

The kind that makes you want to shut this book and say,
I've already failed.

If that is you, stay with me.
Not because you need to be corrected—
but because you deserve to be held.

This is not here to measure you.
It is here to bless you.

To remind you that God is not asking for a perfect past—
He is offering you a redeemed present.
And repair is not a consolation prize.
Repair is one of the most powerful forms of love.

This chapter is for:

the woman with children.
the woman without children.
the woman longing for children.
the woman mothering spiritually, emotionally, relationally.
the woman whose healing will shape the world that follows her.

And before we talk about motherhood in any form,
we have to remember something we began with—
before the fracture,
before the survival,
before the armor.

There is a girl God placed within you—
a part of you made for wonder, play, imagination, beauty, and delight.

There is a girl God placed within you—
a part of you made for wonder, play, imagination, beauty, and
delight.
A part that once lived wide open
before you learned to read the room,
before you learned to make yourself smaller,
before life taught you to brace for what might come.

Motherhood through restoration
is not only about raising children well.

It is also about recovering that girl.
And learning how to keep her alive—
in you,
and in the ones you love.

Because we never want to lose our wonder.

The Shift: Motherhood After Healing

A healing woman mothers differently—
not because she tries harder,
but because she is no longer mothering from pain she didn't
choose.

She no longer grips out of fear—
controlling,
hovering,
bracing for what could go wrong.

She no longer disappears out of duty—
numbing,
over-functioning,
or going silent to keep the peace.

She is present—not perfect.
She is steady—not anxious.
She is attuned—not over-functioning.

Her children do not carry her unmet needs.
Her love does not come with pressure.
Her guidance does not come with fear.

This is what restoration does.

Grace is what makes her safe enough to love.
Grit is what helps her stay present when fear tries to take the
wheel.

It does not make a woman softer in strength—
it makes her *safer in love.*

And when a woman becomes safe within herself,
everything she touches begins to breathe.

This is not about what you did or didn't do.
It is about who you are becoming now.

The Eagle Mother Who Trusts the Wind

There is a moment in nature that has always left me undone.

It happens high above the ground,
far from the noise,
far from safety as we usually define it.

An eagle mother builds her nest not in soft places,
but in high ones—
on cliffs,
on ledges,
places where the wind is strong
and the ground is far away.

She lines the nest carefully when her eaglets are small—
soft feathers,
down,
protection.

She hovers.
She watches.
She feeds.
She guards.

But there comes a day when the eaglet grows restless.

Its wings stretch wider than the nest allows.
Its body no longer fits the place that once held it.

And this is where motherhood changes.

The eagle does not cling
or build higher walls.

She does not keep the nest comfortable forever.

Instead, she does something that looks cruel
to anyone who does not understand trust.

She removes the soft lining.

The nest becomes uncomfortable—
not unsafe, but unsettled.

The eaglet shifts.
Stumbles.
Feels the edge.

And then, at the right moment—
not in anger,
not in fear,
not in abandonment—
the eagle nudges her young out of the nest.

Not to harm.
Not to punish.
But to awaken what was already there.

The eaglet falls.

For a moment, it feels like failure.
Like danger.
Like freefall.

And then—
instinct awakens.

An eaglet is born with wings it has not yet learned to trust.
Its wings are already there—
but flight only emerges when it must trust what was placed
within it.

Wings spread.
Muscles engage.
Air meets feather.

The eaglet does not fall to its death.

It flies.

And here is the part most people miss:

The mother never leaves.
She does not disappear when the eaglet falls.

She soars beneath it—
just below,
just near enough—
ready to catch it if the wings falter.

But she does not fly for it.

This is not abandonment.
This is not neglect.
This is mature love.

This is motherhood that trusts design.

A healed woman mothers this way.

She does not keep her children—
or those she loves—
in nests that no longer fit who they are becoming.

She does not confuse control with care.
She does not mistake fear for protection.

She trusts the wings God placed within them.

And she stays close—
not to rescue from every fall,
but to remind them they were built to rise.

You were released because you were ready.

And if that lands in you with both comfort and grief—
good.

That means your heart is awake.

Because motherhood,
in every form,
is where our deepest fears and our deepest faith often meet.

This kind of motherhood is not limited to raising children.
It shows up in how a woman loves her adult children,
blesses her grandchildren,
steadies a classroom,
builds a community,
carries a calling—
and learns to be gentle with the girl inside herself.

A healed woman learns when to soften the nest
and when to step back.

She learns when to comfort
and when to trust.

She learns that love does not always look like holding tight.

Sometimes, love looks like release.

And the most sacred part?

The eagle never pushes from frustration.
She waits for readiness.

Healing teaches a woman this timing.

She no longer parents from panic.
She no longer reacts from her own unhealed wounds.
She no longer grips because she is afraid of loss.

She mothers from wholeness.

She knows that the same God who designed the wings
also designed the wind.

And she trusts both.

> "Like an eagle that stirs up its nest and hovers over its
> young, spreads its wings, catches them,
> and carries them on its feathers,
> the Lord alone led him."
> —Deuteronomy 32:11–12

Take a breath here.

If you are a mother—
consider where you may be holding tighter than love requires.

If you are a daughter—
consider whether your falling was actually the moment you
learned to fly.

If you are a grandmother—
consider how your healing is creating safer skies
for generations you may never fully see.

And if you are simply a woman becoming whole—
consider this:

You were never pushed out of the nest to fail.
You were released—
because you were ready.

Pain, Identity, and Awakening

Pain has a way of making a woman forget.

When life shatters—
through deception,
disappointment,
neglect,
trauma,
or loss—
a woman forgets who she is.
She forgets who God is.
She forgets what the world once felt like when she lived freely
inside her own skin.

Pain blurs identity.
It muffles radiance.
It covers truth with survival.

When a woman arrives in a counseling room,
she is rarely broken—
she is usually buried.

Buried beneath roles,
expectations,
decades of holding everyone else together,
stories she never asked to carry.

And because pain is loud and identity is quiet,
the story that hurt her starts narrating her life:

This is just who I am now.
This is what life will always feel like.
This is what my children will remember.

But hear me:

Pain is not identity.
Pain is the place where identity gets hidden.

And when a woman fractures, she needs someone—
a counselor, a friend, a mentor, a sister,
or the Holy Spirit—
to sit with her and gently unpack the truth:

How did I get here?
What did this cost me?
Where did I lose myself?
What did I come to believe that God never said?

This unpacking isn't dramatic—
it is **holy** work.

Slow work.

Resurrection work.

Healing is not linear.
It is not fast.
It is certainly not tidy.

And here is the miracle:

If you do not heal,
the story that broke you becomes your identity.

But if you choose to heal,
the story that broke you becomes your testimony.

This is why healing matters—
not only for your story,
not only for your heart,
but for the generations that come after you.

Because healing is inheritance.

And now, as we turn toward motherhood—
whatever motherhood looks like in your life—
hear one of the most sacred truths of the feminine soul:

A healed woman raises a different generation.
Even if the generation she is raising begins with herself.

Healing Before Parenting

Motherhood—
whether expressed through birth,
adoption,
mentoring,
spiritual mothering,
or daily presence—
is often the first place a woman's radiance goes to serve . . .
and the first place it goes to bleed.

We don't become mothers in a vacuum.
We mother out of the stories we carry.
We mother out of the wounds we never named.
We mother out of the beliefs we absorbed when no one was
watching.

Most women step into motherhood
the same way they stepped into womanhood:

In survival,
not abundance.

Most mothers love fiercely—
but mother from places that have never been fully loved.

Most mothers pour deeply—
but pour from wells that were never filled.

And yet—
something miraculous happens when a woman begins to heal.

Her motherhood transforms even before her circumstances do.

Her presence steadies.
Her tenderness returns.
Her fear loosens its grip.
Her voice softens in strength rather than strain.
Her shame releases.
Her joy rises again.

Her boundaries strengthen—
not from anger, but from clarity.

Her love becomes spacious rather than suffocating.

Healing in a woman becomes safety in her home.
Restoration in her heart becomes restoration in her children.

Because here is the truth most women never hear:

You do not need to be a perfect mother.
You only need to be a healing one.

Children do not require flawlessness.

They require **one** thing:

a parent willing to see themselves honestly
and grow slowly, courageously, beautifully with God.

That is enough to reshape a generation.

And for the woman reading this who feels late,
or afraid,
or heavy with regret—
hear me gently:

Repair is powerful.
Humility heals.
Presence can rebuild trust.

If you feel behind,
I want you to hear this plainly:

Love that repairs still counts.
Love that learns still changes the atmosphere.
Love that returns still becomes legacy.

Parenting After Pain: Three Shifts That Change Everything

When healing settles into a woman, her parenting begins to shift—
not in a perfect way,
but in a real way.

Not because her children stop needing her,
but because she stops needing to be everything.

1. You stop parenting from fear and begin parenting from truth.

Fear says: I must control everything.
Truth says: I can guide them without gripping them.

Fear says: I have to protect them from all pain.
Truth says: I will walk with them through it.

Fear-based motherhood is tight,
urgent,
reactive.

Truth-based motherhood is open,
steady,
spacious.

I remember a night—
years after the betrayal,
years after I had clawed my way back to breath—
when one of my kids came into my room long after they should
have been asleep.

My son stood in the doorway,
shoulders slumped,
eyes shining with something he was trying hard to hide.

In the early years of my pain—
before counseling,
before identity work,
before healing had settled into my bones—
I know how I would have responded:

Tight.
Anxious.
Exhausted.
Overfunctioning.

Trying to fix everything with words.

But that night something different happened.

I scooted over on the edge of my bed and simply said,
Come here.

He crawled under the covers and laid his head on my shoulder
the way he did when he was really little.

And instead of lecturing or correcting or teaching him a lesson,
I asked one question:

What is hurting your heart right now?

He exhaled—
a long,
trembling breath—
and started crying.

We didn't have a big conversation.

There was no spiritual breakthrough or perfect parenting moment.
It was quiet,
and small,
and holy in the simplest way.

Later that night,
after he went back to bed,
I sat in the dim light and realized:

This moment would not have been possible before I healed.

Before healing,
I parented some from fear.
From urgency.
From survival.
From the belief that if I didn't hold everything together,
everything would fall apart.

But that night,
something else had entered our home:

Presence.
Softness.
Spaciousness.
Safety.

Healing doesn't make you a perfect parent.
It makes you a safe one.
And a safe mother changes everything.

2. You stop managing behavior and begin shepherding hearts.

Unhealed motherhood often corrects outward actions.
Healing motherhood listens beneath the surface.

Healing mothers begin to ask:

What is my child feeling?
What is this behavior protecting?
What does their heart need from me right now?

Because behavior is communication.
Acting out is often a child's way of saying:

I don't have words for what hurts yet.

There was a day my daughter came home from school with the
kind of heaviness you can feel before she ever speaks a word.

Her backpack dropped to the floor,
and she stood in the kitchen—
small, tired, undone.

I could tell something had happened,
so I did what mothers who love deeply tend to do:

I went straight into fix-it mode.

What happened?
Who said what?
Did you talk to your teacher?
Do I need to call someone?

I started gathering details
the way a mother bear gathers branches—
trying to build something strong enough to protect her child.

But as I asked question after question,
her face didn't relax.
It crumpled.

And in the softest,
most honest voice, she whispered:

Mom . . . will you just cry with me?

Everything in me shifted.

I realized I was trying to solve something she wasn't asking me to solve.

She didn't need answers.
She needed attunement.

So I stopped talking.
Stopped fixing.
Stopped reaching for solutions.

I pulled her close,
wrapped my arms around her,
and let my own tears rise to meet hers.

We cried together—
not in despair,
but in sacred connection.
And I learned something that day:

Holding space for our children is holy work.

Our kids don't always need solutions.
They need companionship in the places that hurt.

They need a mother who can:

sit in silence without rushing them,
feel with them instead of over them,

let them borrow her calm when their world feels shaky,
and offer presence rather than pressure.

Shepherding says,
I'm here with you,
before I'm here to fix anything.

3. You stop disappearing and begin modeling healthy humanity.

Children do not need a perfect mother.
They need a whole one.

When you rest, they learn rest.
When you apologize, they learn humility.
When you have needs, they learn needs are not shameful.
When you feel emotion, they learn emotion is not dangerous.
When you set boundaries, they learn boundaries are love.
When I repair, they learn relationships can be restored.

Some of the holiest moments in my home were the ones where I
sat on the edge of a bed and said:

I'm sorry.
That wasn't about you.
Can we start over?

Those moments didn't weaken my children's trust—
they strengthened it.

Because a mother who can repair teaches a child that love is safe
even when humans are not perfect.

And that, too, changes everything.

One Healing Parent Can Change the Emotional Climate of a Home

There was a long season in my life when the emotional weight of our home felt like it rested entirely on my shoulders.

Not because their father didn't love our children—
but because he was disengaged in ways I couldn't fix.

And I had to make a choice:

I could spend my energy resenting what wasn't there,
or I could pour my energy
into creating what my children needed there.

So I asked myself a question I now ask the women in my office:

What kind of atmosphere do I want my children to remember?

What I wanted most was connection.
And for me, connection always began with play.

So we played.

We rode bikes around the neighborhood until the streetlights
flickered on.
We jumped on the trampoline until we were out of breath,
laughing so hard our sides hurt . . .
or until I peed on myself—
which happened more than once.

My kids thought it was hilarious.
And honestly, so did I.

We danced barefoot in the kitchen.
Made up silly songs.
Built blanket forts and planned scavenger hunts.
Turned ordinary afternoons into small adventures.

Not because I was trying to be the *fun mom*.
But because play creates connection.
And connection opens the door to communication.

Slowly—
almost quietly—
the emotional climate of our home began to shift.

My kids started coming to me with the small things . . .
and then the bigger things.

There was a day one of my kids said to me,
Mom, I feel like I can tell you anything.

And I remember thinking,
This is what a home is built on.

Not perfection.
Not ideal structures.
Not two fully engaged parents.

But one soft, steady, safe parent who keeps showing up.

One parent who listens more than they lecture.
One parent who repairs quickly.
One parent who models humanity.
One parent who becomes their child's emotional landing place.

And I want you to hear this with gentleness:

If you feel alone in your marriage, it will be okay.
If you are a single parent, it will be okay.
If you carry more than your fair share, it will be okay.

Not because that is what you were meant to hold . . .
but because your children can still be safe with you.

Your children do not need perfect parents to be whole.

They need one healing parent who is safe.

One emotionally healthy parent can change the entire emotional climate of a home.

Not by being everything—
but by being present.

Emotional Inheritance: What You Pass Down on Purpose

Children inherit more than genetics.

They inherit how you breathe in the morning.
How you speak to yourself.
How you repair.
How you rest.
How you pray.
How you rise.
Your healing becomes their emotional vocabulary.

This is generational restoration:

not what you pass down by accident—
but what you pass down on purpose.

There are moments in life when healing becomes visible—
not in journals,
not in counseling notes,
but in generations.

I had one of those moments recently.

My youngest daughter—
the one who was just six months old when my world shattered—
sat in her home rocking her newborn daughter,
holding her with a steadiness and softness I didn't have the privilege of giving her at that age.

When she was six months old,
I was walking into a counseling office for the first time,

barely breathing,
barely holding it together—
raising a six-year-old, a four-year-old, a two-year-old, and this
tiny baby on my hip while trying to figure out how to survive
the ruins of the life I once knew.

And now—
twenty-five years later—
I sit on the edge of my daughter's sofa and watch her cradle her
baby girl,
and the emotional climate is different.

Peaceful.
Steady.
Secure.
Soft.

And something in me settles in a way I have never felt before.

This is emotional inheritance.
This is generational healing made visible.

Not perfect lives.
Not perfect parents.

A different starting place.

Healing is slow, holy work—
but its fruit is generational.

Its reward is legacy.

Its impact is a child held in peace
when you were held in pain.

This is the goodness of God across generations.

If you need a moment, take it.

Ask yourself, without judgment:

What did pain make me forget about who I am?

Where have I been parenting—
or living—
from fear instead of identity?

What atmosphere am I creating for the ones I love?

Where might God be inviting me from control into connection?

Healing rarely begins with answers.
It begins with *awareness*.

A Blessing for You

Beloved,

May you know this deep in your bones:

Your healing is holy ground.
Your becoming is not accidental.
Your softness is sacred.

May God gently reveal the unseen fruit of your restoration—
the peace forming in places that once lived on edge,
the tenderness returning to spaces
that learned to harden in order to survive.

May you sense the Holy Spirit beside you
as you mother, nurture, influence, guide, and heal—
whether you mother children, students, communities,
or the younger version of yourself
who is still learning that it is safe to breathe again.

And may you trust this with quiet confidence:

No healing is wasted.
Not one tear.
Not one prayer whispered at 3:00 a.m.

Not one boundary you struggled to hold.
Not one brave step toward wholeness.

Your healing is not only restoring you.
It is restoring the atmosphere of the home you lead,
the relationships you shape,
and the legacy you leave behind.

Because everything that comes next
flows from this truth:

A healed woman becomes a safe place.
And safe places change generations.

And as you keep healing,
keep mothering,
and keep becoming,
may you keep your wonder.

Not the kind that denies pain—
but the kind that remembers delight is still allowed.

The girl God placed in you is not gone.
She is still there.

Wonder is not childish.
It is childlike.

It is the part of you that knows how to delight,
imagine,
and stay open.

And when you protect your wonder,
you give your children—
and the ones you mother—
permission to protect theirs.

You are learning, slowly and beautifully,
how to breathe again.

If you want, take a moment and gently ask yourself:

Where in my life have I traded wonder for survival?

What kind of emotional atmosphere am I creating for those I influence—
through my presence,
not my perfection?

What would it look like to mother from wholeness instead of fear, beginning with myself?

As you begin to remember your wonder,
you may also notice something else rising alongside it.

The strength that kept you alive.
The vigilance that learned to protect.
The part of you that stood guard when softness felt too risky.

That protector does not disappear when healing begins.

She waits to be understood.

Because wholeness is not about choosing between strength and softness.
It is about allowing them to belong together.

And that is where we go next.

Chapter 13

BECOMING WHOLE: REUNITING THE PROTECTOR AND THE RIB

Where grit and grace become partners.

There comes a moment in a woman's healing when she realizes she has lived much of her life split in two.

One part of her became the Protector.
The strong one.
The decisive one.

The woman who learned how to handle what life handed her—often alone.

The other part of her is the Rib.
The woman God designed from the beginning.
The one built for connection,
nurturing,
presence,
and breath.

The one who guards what is sacred,
not by gripping,
but by staying close.

Most women never chose this division.
Life chose it for them.

And if, as you read this,
you feel grief,
or recognition,
or a quiet ache—
pause.

Nothing in this chapter is meant to diagnose you.
Nothing here is meant to imply failure.

This division was not a character flaw.
It was a response to real responsibility,
real loss, and real weight.

Survival does not disqualify you from wholeness.
It explains why wholeness must be gentle.

This is grit—the strength that carried you.
And this is grace—the safety that lets you come home.

A childhood that required emotional caretaking.
A marriage that required vigilance.
A betrayal that required armor.
A career that demanded strength long before tenderness was safe.
A season of single motherhood that required decisiveness,
provision, and constant responsibility.

So she learned to lead with strength—
not because she wanted to,
but because she had to.

And over time, that strength—
necessary and God-given—
began to carry more weight than it was meant to hold alone.

The Woman Who Stopped Asking for Help

I want to tell you about a woman who was not controlling,
not prideful,
and not trying to be everything—
she was simply tired of carrying what had never been shared.

I once sat across from a woman who had not asked for help in
twenty years.
Not once.
Not from her husband.
Not from her children.
Not from her closest friends.

She said, *If I don't do it, it won't get done,*
and then she laughed—
the kind of laugh that tries to hide the ache beneath it.

She wasn't prideful.
She was exhausted.

Her family adored her,
but they had no idea she was drowning
because she had never given them the gift of knowing her need.

Her over-functioning had become its own wound:

no one poured into her
because she had never learned how to make room to receive.

She wasn't invincible.
She was empty.

And what she needed was not to try less—
but to be held enough to receive more.

This chapter is not about laying down strength.
It is about letting strength *rest somewhere safe.*

It is an invitation to become whole again—
not by rejecting the Protector or romanticizing softness,
but by allowing God to reunite what survival once separated.

Honoring the Armor

Before anything else, we must say this clearly:

Your Protector is not the enemy.
She kept you alive.
She held the line.
She stepped forward when no one else did.

Scripture honors this kind of strength:

> "A sensible person sees danger and takes cover."
> —Proverbs 22:3

But what protected you in one season can confine you in another.

Armor that is never set down eventually becomes a cage.

And God, in His kindness,
does not shame us for wearing armor—
He invites us to take it off when it is no longer required.

The Rib Still Lives in You

The Rib—
the feminine strength God built into you—
was never erased.

She went quiet because it wasn't safe to be visible.

She is the part of you that:

breathes life rather than holding breath,
nurtures connection rather than managing outcomes,
stays present rather than bracing for impact,
values intimacy over performance,
carries wonder alongside wisdom.

She does not return through effort.
She returns through safety.

And safety is not something you force.

It is something you allow to grow—
slowly, relationally, without pressure.

A Holy Tension: Strength and Tenderness in the Same Day

A friend of mine has worked in radio for over thirty years.

Radio is a high-pressure field—
not because of gender,
but because of what it demands:

decisiveness,
stamina,
authority,
thick skin.

The industry has changed rapidly,
becoming more digital,
more competitive,
more unforgiving.

To survive,
she shows up every day strong,
prepared, and unflappable.

For eight hours, she leads with strength.
Then she drives home to a small house where her son is waiting.
And she takes a breath.

Because the voice that commands meetings cannot be the voice
that tucks a child into bed.

The strength that manages deadlines cannot be the posture that
listens to fears,
questions,
and longings.

So she loosens the armor.
Not perfectly.
Not always easily.

She shifts from directing to listening.
From solving to sitting.
From guarding to holding.

Some nights she says, I *feel like I've lived two lives in one day.*

It is a tension—
but it is not a failure.

It is a holy tension.

Her strength keeps the lights on.
Her tenderness keeps her son's heart open.

This is grit and grace stewarded in the same body,
in the same life.

Stewarding Feminine Strength

Healing opens the door.
Stewardship determines the atmosphere.

Scripture is clear:

"Guard your heart above all else,
for it is the source of life."
—Proverbs 4:23

"Pay careful attention,
then, to how you live."
—Ephesians 5:15

God created you with intention.
He restores you with patience.
And He invites you to steward what He has formed.

For many women,
stewarding feminine strength looks like choosing spaces where
softness is safe:

holding a grandchild,
shepherding children's hearts,
serving the elderly or vulnerable,
working with children,
volunteering in places
where presence matters more than performance.

These are not small things.
They are holy practices of nurture.

And stewardship also means choosing community wisely.

Scripture does not shy away from influence:

"Do not be deceived:
Bad company corrupts good morals."
—1 Corinthians 15:33

"The one who walks with the wise will become wise."
— Proverbs 13:20

This is not judgment.
It is discernment.

Anger multiplies anger.
Fear multiplies fear.
But healing multiplies healing.

A woman becoming whole needs people who will tell her the truth with love—
who will call her up,
not just comfort her where she is.

Accountability is not control.
It is protection.

Vulnerability as Holy Strength

Vulnerability is one of the clearest expressions of feminine strength.

And it often shows up where the stakes are highest—
inside relationships.

There were years in my marriage when my husband was not showing up well,
and all the signs pointed to his struggle with addiction.

This was not a season of unchecked danger or coercion,
nor a context where my safety was at risk.

It was simply a season where safety was imperfect, yet still possible.

As I continued to grow in my own journey of healing,
I began to understand something important about myself:

For me to feel open to physical and sexual intimacy,
I needed emotional and spiritual connection first.

I love physical touch—
but not when it always leads to sex.

So I chose to be vulnerable by naming what I needed—
knowing that asking itself carried risk,
and that I might be misunderstood or shut down.

My choice emerged from a context where emotional and
physical safety were slowly being restored.

This is not a model for relationships where vulnerability is
punished or ignored.

I asked for play—
volleyball,
tennis,
walks.

I asked for non-sexual time together in the shower where we
could talk without children around us.

I asked for massages that did not lead to sex.

This took courage.
It took honesty.
It created tension.
And it required a learning curve for both of us.

Over time, it contributed to a growing sense of safety.

And as emotional and spiritual connection
deepened outside the bedroom,
physical intimacy within it became richer,
freer, and more mutual.

I did not wait for him to lead,
not because I was certain,
but because I was learning to listen honestly to myself.

I did not manipulate.
I did not demand an outcome.

I named what I needed—
without knowing how it would be received—
and trusted God with the response.

For me, this was stewardship.
It did not feel brave or clean in the moment—
it felt risky, exposing, and uncertain.

A Gentle Word to the Woman Reading

Before you read anything into that story that feels like pressure,
I want to pause and speak directly to you.

If you carry trauma around touch—
childhood sexual abuse,
assault,
violation,
or experiences where your body was not honored—
this story may make your skin tighten instead of soften.

And if that's you,
I want you to hear this clearly:

I see you.

I have sat with countless women whose bodies learned early that
touch was not safe.
Women whose nervous systems learned to brace instead of
receive.
Women who learned to disconnect from their bodies in order to
survive.

If physical touch has felt confusing,
consuming,
or unsafe for you;
if sex has felt like something you endure rather than enjoy;
if your body learned to tense because touch always led

somewhere you weren't ready to go,
nothing about your response means you are broken.

Often, it means your body learned how to protect your heart.

Your response makes sense.
Your caution makes sense.
Your pace matters.

Healing is not a formula.
It is a relationship.
And the timing of that healing is different for every woman.

What I am sharing here is not an instruction.
It is not an expectation.
And it is not a measure of your growth.

It is simply my story—
one woman stewarding her needs honestly within her marriage.

Your story,
your safety,
and your timing may look very different.

Healing never requires you to override your own sense of safety.

Your worth is not measured by how open you are,
how healed you feel,
or how quickly your body responds.

God is not timing you.

As you heal, you get to come back into your body on your terms.

You get to learn what safety feels like again.
You get to say no when something feels wrong.
You get to pause, pull back, set boundaries,
and listen to what your body is telling you.

That is not weakness.
That is wisdom.

Feminine strength does not mean forcing yourself to be open.
It does not mean pushing past discomfort to prove growth.

It means honoring truth in your body
and letting God restore safety there—
slowly,
gently,
faithfully.

You do not owe anyone access to your body.
You do not have to push yourself into vulnerability
before safety is present.

Stewardship looks different for every woman.
Healing unfolds at different speeds.

And as healing unfolds, something holy becomes possible:

You may one day experience touch
not as obligation,
not as performance,
not as something taken from you—
but as something chosen.

Safe.
Connecting.
Life-giving.

But there is no rush.

No timeline.
No comparison.

My hope is not that you do what I did.
My hope is that you feel permission
to listen to your body,

honor your needs,
and trust that God meets you with patience and care
right where you are.

Your healing belongs to you.

And God is deeply attentive
to every step of your becoming.

Why Feminine Strength Requires Gospel Community

One of the most overlooked truths about healing is this:

You cannot steward your feminine design in isolation.

Not because you are weak—
but because you were never designed to mature alone.

Scripture never frames wholeness as a solo project.

From the beginning, God said,

> "It is not good for man to be alone—"
> Genesis 2:18

And that truth extends far beyond marriage.

Women need women.
Not just companionship—
but *formation.*

Not women who simply echo feelings back to us,
but women who help us discern what is true.

Because we live in a world that increasingly mistakes intensity
for truth,
and emotion for authority.

A world where feelings are elevated above facts.

Where pain becomes identity.
Where anger is normalized.
Where healing is often confused with venting.

And while feelings matter—
deeply—
they were never meant to lead.

Scripture is clear:

> "The heart is more deceitful than anything else,
> and incurable . . . who can understand it?"
> —Jeremiah 17:9

> "But speaking the truth in love,
> let us grow in every way into him who is the head—
> Christ."
> —Ephesians 4:15

Truth and love belong together.

Calling Each Other Up—Not Just Out

Gospel community is not about being surrounded by people who always agree with you.

It's about being surrounded by people who love you enough to tell you the truth.

Women who:

hold your pain without letting it harden into bitterness,
validate your grief without feeding your resentment,
listen compassionately—and then ask the harder question,
sit with you in the mess—but don't let you stay stuck there.

This is what Scripture means when it says:

> "As iron sharpens iron, so one person sharpens another."
> —Proverbs 27:17

Sharpening isn't gentle.
But it is loving.

It requires trust,
It requires humility,
and a shared commitment to growth—not just relief.

Why Discernment Matters in Community

Not every gathering of women is healing.

Some spaces keep us:

rehearsing the same wounds,
reinforcing fear,
validating anger without transformation,
bonding over disappointment rather than hope.

Scripture does not shame discernment—it commands it:

> "Walk with the wise and become wise."
> —Proverbs 13:20

> "Do not be deceived:
> Bad company corrupts good morals."
> —1 Corinthians 15:33

This is not about judging other women.
It is about **stewarding your heart.**

And stewardship here does not mean making sudden changes.

It begins with noticing how you feel when you leave a space—
more grounded,
or more stirred.

More clear, or more confused.
Awareness comes before action.

If you are surrounded by constant anger, anger will shape you.
If you are surrounded by despair, despair will settle in.
If you are surrounded by women who live only in their feelings,
clarity will erode.

But when you surround yourself with women who hold grit *and*
grace together—
women who know suffering *and* hope,
truth *and* tenderness,
repentance *and* restoration—
your own life begins to steady.

The Kind of Tribe That Protects Feminine Strength

The community that nurtures feminine design looks like this:

Women who pray before they react,
Women who tell you when fear is driving the bus,
Women who sit with you when it hurts and ask where God is
inviting you to grow,
Women who understand that the gospel is often messy before it
is freeing,
Women who don't rush healing—but also don't avoid truth.

These women don't just have your back.
They have your ***becoming***.

They don't just call you out.
They call you *up*—into courage, clarity, humility, and hope.

A Holy, Messy Tension

Gospel community is rarely neat.

It is holy—and often uncomfortable.
Safe—but not permissive.
Loving—but not indulgent.

It holds this tension:

Grace that covers you.
Truth that forms you.

And when women walk this way together,
something powerful happens.

The Protector no longer has to stand alone.
The Rib no longer has to hide.

Strength finds rest.
Softness finds safety.

And wholeness becomes possible—
not because we perfected ourselves,
but because we allowed God to shape us together.

The Gospel Holds Strength and Tenderness Together

Jesus does not ask women to choose between grit and grace.
He embodies both.

He is the Lion and the Lamb.
Truth and tenderness.
Authority and compassion.

In Him, strength no longer has to stand alone.
In Him, softness is no longer unsafe.

This is why integration does not happen through effort—
it happens through reorientation.

Again and again, we return to Christ.
Again and again, we allow Him to reorder us.
Again and again, we let strength rest under love.

What Holy Community Actually Looks Like

For twelve years, I led a women's support group.
But even saying led feels imprecise.

I showed up each week prepared, prayerful, and open—
but what unfolded in that room was never something I could
manufacture.

Week after week,
women came carrying stories of betrayal,
loss,
addiction,
grief,
exhaustion,
and quiet despair.

They came with their guard up, their hearts tender, their lives
cracked open.

And something sacred happened there.

Not because of my words.
Not because of a curriculum.
Not because anyone had the answers.

But because the Holy Spirit showed up.

Often, the most powerful moments came in the silence—
when no one rushed to fix,
when no one offered advice,
when no one tried to spiritualize the pain away.

We learned to wait.

To sit in the tension of not knowing what to say.
To trust that God was already moving beneath the surface.
To let tears speak when words failed.

And in those moments, I watched women soften.
Walls came down.
Armor loosened.
Breath returned.

We laughed—
deeply, unexpectedly.

We cried—
the kind of crying that cleanses rather than collapses.
And somehow, in that ordinary room, heaven felt close.

It was a glimpse of what the Church is meant to be.

Not **polished.**
Not **performative.**
Not **hurried.**

But **holy.**

As Dr. Dan Allender often reminds caregivers, we cannot
lead others into freedom we have not been willing to pursue
ourselves[1].

And that truth shaped me more than any leadership training
ever could.

Leading that group did not elevate me above anyone else in the room.

It humbled me.

I learned that facilitation is not control—it is *attunement.*

Not directing outcomes—but discerning movement.
Not filling space with words—but honoring the work God was
already doing.

I learned to lead with a limp.

To resist the urge to rescue.
To trust silence.
To believe that transformation is the Holy Spirit's work—
not mine.

And in watching God heal others,
I found myself reminded and reinforced in the healing work I
had already done—
and God was still doing.

That is the power of gospel community.

Not women telling each other what they want to hear.
But women staying present long enough for truth to rise.

Not bypassing pain—
but allowing God to meet us inside it.

Not pretending to be whole—
but becoming whole together.

This is the kind of community that forms women.
This is the kind of accountability that doesn't shame, but
steadies.

This is the holy tension where grit and grace meet.

And it is here—
in shared vulnerability,
shared hope,
shared waiting—
that the feminine soul learns she is safe again.

This is what happens
when women choose presence over performance,
truth over comfort,
and community over isolation.

And it is from this kind of soil—
not striving,
not self-protection—
that wholeness begins to grow.

Becoming Whole

You are not becoming someone new.

You are remembering someone ancient—
the woman God built from the rib,
close to the heart,
near the breath,
designed to guard what is sacred and carry what is holy.

Wholeness is not perfection.
It is presence.

It is strength that knows when to stand
and tenderness that knows when to speak.

It is vulnerability rooted in wisdom.
It is accountability wrapped in grace.

And it is lived—
not alone—
but in community,
under the steady care of a God who restores all that survival once
divided.

Take a breath.

You don't have to choose between strength and softness anymore.

They belong together.

Before we move forward, let's pause.
Not to solve anything—just to notice.

You don't need to answer all of these.
You don't need to write anything down.

Simply notice what rises.

Where in my life have I been living primarily from protection
rather than presence?
No judgment—just awareness.

What part of me has been strong for a very long time?
And what might she need right now?

When I imagine strength and softness working together inside
me, what do I feel—relief, fear, grief, hope?

Who helps me stay aligned with truth and love—
not just comfort or approval?
Who calls me up, not out?

When a woman begins to reunite the protector and the rib,
something quiet but significant happens inside her.

Strength loosens its grip.
Softness edges closer.

Long-held tensions rise to the surface—
not to overwhelm her,
but to be acknowledged.

Integration is holy work.
And holy work requires rest.

You do not integrate by trying harder.

You integrate by staying present long enough for God to bring
things back together.

If this chapter stirred something in you—
memories, emotions, tenderness, resistance—
that is not a sign you have gone too far.

It is a sign that something true has been touched.

You do not need to sort it out.
You do not need to respond well.
You do not need to decide what any of it means yet.

This is not the moment for action.
It is the moment for *settling*.

Before the soul can move forward,
the body needs to know it is safe.

Before identity can deepen,
the nervous system must be allowed to exhale.

Not to analyze what opened—
but to give it somewhere to land.
So we pause here.

And I want to pray for you:

> God of breath and becoming,
> You see the woman reading these words.
> You see the strength she learned to carry—
> the armor she put on when love required vigilance,
> the tenderness she protected when the world felt unsafe.
>
> You have never been confused by her strength.
> You have never been threatened by her questions.
> You have never been distant from her ache.
>
> So we ask gently:
>
> Would You meet her in the places where survival once split
> her in two?
>
> Where the protector learned to stand alone,
> teach her that she does not have to hold everything anymore.

Where the Rib learned to grow quiet,
remind her that softness is not dangerous in Your presence.

Reunite what pain separated.
Not through force.
Not through effort.
But through safety.

Let strength rest under love.
Let tenderness rise without fear.
Let her body know it is no longer bracing for impact.
Let her soul remember that it was made for connection, not
constant readiness.

If there are memories stirred that she cannot name,
hold them for her.

If there is grief she does not yet have language to name,
receive it.

If there is resistance protecting something fragile,
honor it.

You are not in a hurry.

Teach her how to listen—
to her body,
to her limits,
to Your Spirit.

Teach her how to trust that she does not have to earn rest.
Teach her how to believe that being held is not weakness.

And as she continues this journey—
not perfectly,
not quickly,
but honestly—
surround her with people who hold truth and love together.

People who steady her when fear rises.
People who call her forward without pushing her past herself.

May she know this, deep in her bones:

She is not becoming someone new.
She is being restored to who You always designed her to be.

Strong and soft.
Wise and open.
Rooted and free.

We place her back into Your care now—
not to fix herself,
not to figure everything out,
but to rest.

Amen.

The girl inside you has been listening.
The protector inside you has been working hard.

Both deserve rest.

What comes next is not another demand.
It is an invitation.

An invitation to slow down.
To receive instead of produce.
To be held instead of holding everything together.

We are not moving into effort.
We are moving into room.

PART VI

THE THRESHOLD

The invitation to sit.

Chapter 14

MAKING ROOM FOR
THE GIRL INSIDE

Regulation. Safety. Receiving.

After the work of integration, the body asks for rest.
After strength has spoken, tenderness needs space to land.

After the Protector and the Rib have been brought back into
conversation,
the body needs a place where nothing more is required.

That is where we are now.

Before anything is asked of you, something must be given:

Space.

Not the kind of space you have learned to create by pushing
everything down and holding yourself together—
but the kind that allows you to soften without collapsing.

The weeping willow has always felt like a living picture of this.
Its branches droop like grief—like mourning given shape.
And yet it does not shatter.

It bends.
It endures.
It yields to the wind without losing its root.
It carries resilience in its structure—renewal woven into its design.

Growing up in Florida,
I was always drawn to weeping willows.
Not as an idea—almost as a refuge.

Those long, feminine branches felt like flowing curtains, like mercy.

I loved how you could stand beneath them
and suddenly,
the world got quieter—
like the tree became a kind of guardian,
making room to breathe.

A place to hide without disappearing.
A place to be held without being fixed.

It grows at the edge of land and water—
at the threshold—
where one world meets another.

Not because it is fragile,
but because it is made for places that require both strength and
surrender.

And when it is cut back,
it is known for returning—
regenerating, rising again.

Not by force—
by design.

This is what your body is learning here:

how to bend without breaking,
how to grieve without collapsing,
how to be soft without becoming unsafe.

Many women arrive at this point in the story feeling tired but not knowing why.

And many carry a quiet shame for that tiredness—
especially when they have been mothers to others for so long.

Not tired from doing too little—
tired from doing too much for too long.

Tired from being strong where softness was never protected.
Tired from holding their breath through whole seasons of life.
Tired from carrying responsibility in places where companionship was meant to live.

If that is you, pause here and notice something simple:

You are still here.

Your body carried you.
Your heart kept beating.
Your soul did not leave you.

The girl inside you survived.

She learned how to be quiet when quiet felt safer.
She learned how to be strong when no one else could be.
She learned how to read the room, anticipate needs, smooth edges, and hold the center.

And none of that made her weak.

But it did make her tired.

That was grit.
And now grace is making room for you to rest.

This chapter is not about changing her.
It is about making room for her to finally rest.

So before we go any further, let's slow down.

Take a breath that doesn't need to go anywhere.

Not a deep breath that performs calm—
just an honest one.

Notice where your body is holding itself together right now.

Your shoulders.
Your jaw.
Your stomach.
Your chest.

You don't need to fix it.
You don't need to relax on command.

Just notice.

Many women were never taught how to feel safe inside their
own bodies.

Safety was something external—
dependent on mood, approval, harmony, performance.

So the nervous system adapted.

It stayed alert.
It stayed ready.
It learned to brace.

And bracing, over time, begins to feel normal.

But the body was never meant to live in constant readiness.

It was meant to move between effort and rest,
giving and receiving,
strength and softness.

This is where receiving begins—
not with understanding,
but with **permission.**

Permission to stop proving.
Permission to stop holding everything upright.
Permission to stop being the one who has it all together.

God does not meet you here to correct you.

He meets you here to **hold you.**
Not as a project.
Not as a problem.
But as a daughter who has carried more than she should have
had to.

Scripture says:

> "As a mother comforts her son,
> so I will comfort you,
> and you will be comforted in Jerusalem."
> —Isaiah 66:13

And:

> "The Lord is near to the brokenhearted;
> he saves those crushed in spirit."
> —Psalm 34:18

Near does not mean demanding.
Near does not mean fixing.

Near means present.

If you listen closely, you may notice how unfamiliar that feels—
being held without being evaluated.

Most women have experienced help
that came with conditions,
support that arrived with expectations,
care that required gratitude, productivity,
or improvement in return.

So even kindness can feel dangerous.

But this is different.

This is the kind of safety that does not rush you forward.
The kind that does not need you to explain yourself.
The kind that allows the girl inside you to come closer without
fear.

The girl inside you still knows what safety can feel like—
even if it has been a long time.

She remembers moments of softness:

Being wrapped in a towel after a bath.
Falling asleep on the couch.
The quiet relief of someone else taking over.

Sometimes, she remembers being cared for without being assessed.

That memory lives in your body, not your mind.

And God knows how to reach it.
He does not stand over you, asking you to do better.

He kneels beside you and says,

You don't have to hold this alone anymore.

This is the place where goodness is allowed to land.

Not all at once.
Not dramatically.

Just enough to be felt.

Goodness landing might look like your shoulders dropping half an inch.
It might look like tears that surprise you.
It might look like nothing at all—just a quiet sense that you don't need to brace quite as hard.

That is enough.

This is not the chapter where you revisit every wound.

That work has already been honored.

This is the chapter where your system learns that it is allowed to stop scanning for danger—
at least for a moment.

Here, God prepares a room within you.

Not a room you have to clean first.
Not a room you have to earn access to.

A place where the girl inside you is not rushed, corrected, or improved.

A room where she is simply welcome.

Jesus once said:

> "Come to me,
> all of you who are weary and burdened,
> and I will give you rest."
> —Matthew 11:28

Rest is not reward.
Rest is relationship.

Rest is stewardship—
the gentle tending of what God entrusted to you:

your body, your limits, your heart—
not by striving, but by receiving.

You may notice resistance as you sit here.

That is normal.

The protector in you learned its job well.
It kept you alive.

It deserves respect, not dismissal.

So if part of you is watching carefully, waiting to see what
happens next—
thank it.

Let it know this is not a trap.

Nothing is about to be demanded of you.

This chapter is the pause before participation.
The inhale before movement.
The stillness before the next step.

You are not behind.
You are not failing.
You are not doing this wrong.

You are learning how to receive.
Receiving does not undo your strength—
it gives it somewhere safe to rest.

And for many women,
that is the bravest work of all.

So stay here a little longer than feels efficient.

Let the room hold you.
Let God be near without asking anything in return.

We will move forward soon enough.

For now—
you may rest.

You don't need to answer these.
You don't need to understand them.
Simply notice what feels true.

What does rest feel like in my body right now—
familiar,
unfamiliar,
comforting,
uncomfortable?

What part of me has been holding everything together?
And what might it be like to let her rest—
just for this moment?

If God were looking at me with tenderness instead of
expectation, what might He want me to know right now?

You are not meant to carry clarity yet.
You are meant to be held.

Rest does not end the journey.
It **grounds** it.

When a woman is given room to breathe,
something begins to settle inside her.

Not answers.
Not strategies.
But steadiness.

The girl inside you does not stay hidden when she is welcomed.
She softens.
She listens.
She remembers.

And from that place of rest, something quiet begins to rise.

A different way of showing up.
A different way of leading.
A different way of loving.

Not from pressure—
but from presence.

A Prayer for Rest and Receiving

God who comes near,
we are here now—
not to accomplish,
not to understand,
not to fix.

We are here because You are near.
You see the woman who has been strong for a very long time.
You see the girl inside her who learned to wait quietly.
You see the protector who stayed alert so others could rest.

And You are not asking any of them to do more.

Would You let her body know it is safe right now?

Not safe forever.
Not safe in theory.
Just safe enough for this moment.

If her breath feels shallow, meet her there.
If her muscles won't soften yet, stay with her anyway.
If tears come, hold them.

If nothing comes, that is okay too.

Teach her that rest is not something she earns.
Teach her that receiving is not selfish.
Teach her that being held does not make her weak.

If she has been mothering everyone else,
comfort her with a mother's tenderness now.

If she has carried responsibility that was never hers,
set it down gently for her.

If the girl inside her is still unsure it's safe,
tell her she is welcome.

She does not need to perform.
She does not need to explain.
She does not need to be brave.

Let goodness land where it can.
Let safety take root slowly.

Let her know—
without words—
that she is not alone.

We trust You with the pace.
We trust You with what is next.

For now, we rest.
Amen.

What comes next is not about doing more.

It is about noticing what your healing is already touching
beyond you.

Because a woman who has learned to receive
inevitably changes the atmosphere around her.

The next chapter is not about striving forward.
It is about what your restoration makes possible.

For others.
For generations.
For the legacy you are already shaping—
whether you see it yet or not.

Chapter 15

RADIANCE RESTORED

From healing to inheritance.

Healing does not end with you.
It settles within you.

It softens what was once tight.
It steadies what once lived on edge.

And then—often without your noticing—
it begins to move outward.

Not loudly.
Not urgently.
Not as a performance to be measured or displayed.

But as presence.

By the time a woman reaches this place,
something subtle and sacred has shifted.

She no longer lives in constant repair mode.
She no longer scans herself for what still needs fixing.
She no longer waits for permission to rest inside her own skin.

She has learned how to breathe again.
Not the shallow breathing of survival—
but the steady, spacious breathing of safety.

She has learned how to listen without panic.
How to notice without judgment.
How to let God meet her where she actually is,
not where she thinks she should be by now.

And that changes everything.

Because healing was never meant to stop at relief.
It was meant to return you to yourself.

Healing is not about becoming someone new.
It is about remembering—
again and again—
who God created you to be before fear became loud
and before survival demanded armor.

This is the long arc of God's work in a woman's life.
Not instant transformation.
Not flawless arrival.
But faithful restoration over time.

Scripture tells us:

> "I am sure of this,
> that he who started a good work in you
> will carry it on to completion
> until the day of Christ Jesus."
> —Philippians 1:6

Completion does not mean perfection on this side of heaven.
It means God is not finished with you.
Not today.
Not tomorrow.
Not in this season.

You are still becoming.

And in that becoming,
you are being entrusted with something sacred:

Your life.
Your presence.
Your influence.
Your quiet, steady radiance.

What you carry now is not pressure—
but inheritance in motion.

Legacy Is Not Perfection—It Is Wisdom

So many women think legacy is something they leave behind
after they get it all right.

But legacy is not about flawlessness.
It is about **wisdom lived honestly.**

Legacy is what children, friends, students,
and communities absorb simply by being near a woman who has
done her healing work.

A woman who knows when to rest,
who knows how to repair,
who no longer confuses control with love,
who offers safety instead of solutions,
who listens without rushing,
who stays present instead of disappearing.

This is how healing reshapes generations.

Not through lectures.
Not through managing outcomes.
But through *atmosphere*.

Children don't inherit what we say as much as they inherit **how it feels to be with us.**

And a healed woman creates a different emotional climate wherever she goes.

Legacy is not what you leave behind someday.
It is what settles into a room when you walk into it now.

Spiritual Motherhood: Presence, Not Biology

This is why motherhood is far bigger than biology.

This includes the woman who never became a mother,
or the woman who lost one,
and the woman who carries grief or regret around how she mothered.

Every woman mothers in some way.

Through presence,
guidance,
hospitality,
mentoring,
quiet faithfulness,
creating spaces where others can exhale.

Spiritual motherhood is the act of saying,
often without words,
You are safe here.
You don't have to perform.
You don't have to disappear.
You don't have to earn love.

And here is the quiet truth:

You cannot offer what you have not first received.

Which means the most powerful thing you will ever give others is the fruit of your own restoration.

Your children.
Your grandchildren.
The women God places beside you.
The girls who are watching you from a distance.

They don't need you to be impressive.
They need you to be **whole**.

Radiance Lived, Not Performed

Radiance does not require effort.

It is not something you put on.
It is something that returns when you stop hiding.

Radiance is what happens when strength and softness are no longer at war inside you.

That's grit and grace held together—
strength that endures and love that lets you rest.

When you no longer abandon yourself to be accepted.
When your body, heart, and spirit begin to agree again.

You don't have to announce it.
People feel it.

It shows up in how your shoulders rest.
In how your voice sounds when you're not rushing.
In how others exhale around you.

A woman who embodies her radiance changes rooms without trying.

She lowers anxiety,
steadies chaos,

invites honesty,
and makes space for others to tell the truth.

And she does this not because she is special in the way the world
defines special—
but because she is **fully herself.**

There is no one like you.

There never has been.
There never will be.

The particular way God formed your heart,
your story,
your nervous system,
your compassion,
your strength—
it is not accidental.

And when you live from that place,
your healing becomes inheritance.

Carrying Restoration Forward

Nothing is being demanded of you here.

You are not being sent out to do more.
You are not being asked to become a guide, a leader, or a healer
if that is not your calling.

You are simply being trusted.

Trusted to live what has been restored,
to keep returning to God when you lose your way,
to keep choosing truth over fear,
to keep softening when hardness feels safer.

This is the invitation Jesus offers:

> "Remain in me, and I in you.
> Just as a branch is unable to produce fruit by itself
> unless it remains on the vine,
> neither can you unless you remain in me."
> —John 15:4

Abiding is not striving.
It is staying connected.

And as you abide, your life becomes a quiet testimony—
not of perfection,
but of faithfulness.

Beloved,
you have what it takes to continue this journey.

Not because you are strong enough—
but because God is faithful enough.

You are not late.
You are not behind.
You are not missing something everyone else figured out.

You are ***becoming.***

May you continue to reorient yourself—again and again—
to who God created you to be.

May you trust that the healing you tend today
will become the peace someone else gets to live in tomorrow.

May you know, deep in your bones,
that your radiance matters.

And may you live the rest of your days
not trying to prove your worth,
but resting in the truth that you were always worth restoring.

Until the day you are fully healed in heaven,
may you walk this earth as a woman
who has learned how to breathe, to receive,
and to love from wholeness.

Radiance was never lost.
It was waiting—
in your body,
in your breath,
in the slow unfolding
of your becoming.

EPILOGUE:
A BLESSING FOR THE
FEMININE SOUL

Faith that can breathe.

Take a breath.

Not because you've reached the end,
but because you don't have to carry anything forward right now.

Let your shoulders soften.
Let your jaw unclench.
Let your body notice it is safe enough,
in this moment,
to exhale.

This book was never meant to rush you toward a result.

It was meant to walk beside you until you remembered
how to stand inside yourself again.

Grit and grace were never meant to compete inside you.
They were meant to hold hands.

Grit carried you when grace felt far away.
Grace met you when grit finally got to rest.

Both have served you.
Neither defines you.

Together, they led you here—
to a faith that no longer holds its breath.

What defines you is this:

You are God's beloved.

Not because you healed well.
Not because you stayed strong.
Not because you figured anything out.

But because He chose you.

> "I have loved you with an everlasting love;
> therefore, I have continued to extend faithful love to you."
> —Jeremiah 31:3

Faith was never meant to suffocate you.
It was meant to give you air.

A faith that breathes does not demand constant strength.

It does not confuse holiness with exhaustion.
It does not require you to disappear in order to belong.

A faith that breathes invites you to rest
inside the love that has already claimed you.

So as you close these pages,
do not ask yourself what you should do next.

Ask yourself something gentler:

What feels true now?
What feels softer?
What feels possible?

And trust that God is at work
even when nothing feels dramatic.

You will forget again.
You will tighten again.
You will reach for armor when fear flares.

And when you do,
you are not failing.

You are human.

Simply return.

Return to breath.

Return to truth.
Return to belovedness.

Return to the girl God placed in you
before the noise,
before the fracture,
before survival taught you to hide.

She is not fragile.

She is not naive.

She is wise,
resilient,
and known by God.

And she is still there.

You do not leave this book with answers.

You leave it with permission.

Blessing:

> "May the Lord bless you and protect you;
> may the Lord make His face shine upon you
> and be gracious to you;
> may the Lord look with favor on you
> and give you peace."
> —Numbers 6:24–26

May your strength soften without disappearing.
May your tenderness grow without fear.

May your life reflect a holiness
that looks like presence, not perfection.

And may you remember this, always:

Radiance was never lost.
It was waiting.

And it will keep waiting for you
every time you choose to come home to yourself—
and to Him again—
until the day you are fully home in Him.

Acknowledgments

Every book is written by one set of hands, but no book is ever born from one life alone.

I carry deep gratitude for the thousands of women I have walked beside for nearly two decades . . . women who entrusted me with sacred space and shared stories of grief, courage, healing, and hope.

Your vulnerability and resilience helped shape the heart of this book. Though the stories here have been carefully protected and changed to preserve privacy, the wisdom and courage you carried are woven quietly throughout these pages.

To Kelly, Becky, Langston, Paul, Scott, Janice, Sherri, and Angela . . . thank you. Your discipleship, mentorship, accountability, counsel, and wisdom have shaped my life in ways too deep for words. You helped steady me, heal me, and call me forward, and your imprint remains on my life and this work.

To my editor, Stacy K. . . . thank you for your thoughtful encouragement and steady care as you helped me keep refining this manuscript until it finally became what it was meant to be.

Rylo Creative . . . thank you for the beautiful illustrations that quietly echo the themes of restoration, gentleness, and breath throughout this book, and for the steady encouragement you offered along the way.

To my friends, colleagues, church, and community . . . you have been a lifeline. Your presence, prayers, and support have carried me more than you know.

Terri Guffin, my fellow Jacksonville, Florida, girl and my lifelong friend since our days at Samford . . . thank you for witnessing my life through every joy, fracture, and restoration. Thank you for loving me with the rare kind of friendship that stays, laughs with me, understands without explanation, and holds a story with tenderness and grace.

Mom and Dad, you walked through this manuscript with me and have been a redemptive part of my restoration story. You encouraged me, blessed me, and prayed for me and with me as this work found its way into the world. Your love has been one of God's kindnesses to me.

To my sisters and my family, who have loved me through every season of this work . . . thank you for your patience, your encouragement, and your belief in what God has placed in my heart.

Ryland, Tal, Gabe, and Keller . . . you are among my greatest treasures on this earth. Hudson and Hannah, you are answered prayers. And to my first grandchild, Lively Grace, who in many ways helped awaken this work . . . we are just getting started. I love each of you so deeply. You keep me growing, stretching, and returning again and again to who God created me to be. I look forward to the legacy we will continue building together for generations to come.

And finally, to the Lord . . . whose love met me at the age of eight and has held me ever since, whose kindness has steadied me through every season, and who still meets us in our weakness and gently restores what life has fractured . . .

Every page of this book rests in His grace.

Endnotes

Chapter 1

1. John Eldredge and Stasi Eldredge, *Captivating: Unveiling the Mystery of a Woman's Soul* (Nashville: Thomas Nelson, 2005).

Chapter 2

1. For discussion of the Hebrew word *ezer* in Genesis 2:18 as a term of strength, aid, and essential partnership, see Carmen Joy Imes, *Bearing God's Name: Why Sinai Still Matters* (Downers Grove, IL: IVP Academic, 2019).

Chapter 6

1. Dan B. Allender, writings on early attachment, trauma, and the formation of pre-verbal interpretive patterns.

2. Curt Thompson, writings on attunement, being seen, and interpersonal neurobiology.

Chapter 9

1. For discussion of the Hebrew verb *banah* in Genesis 2:22, often translated "built," see standard Hebrew lexicons and commentaries on Genesis 2.

2. For discussion of the Hebrew word *tzelah* in Genesis 2:21–22, often translated "rib" but elsewhere rendered "side," including its use in tabernacle and temple contexts, see standard Hebrew

lexicons and Old Testament studies on Genesis and sanctuary imagery.

3. For discussion of the phrase *ezer kenegdo* in Genesis 2:18 and its implications of corresponding strength and partnership, see Hebrew word studies on Genesis 2:18.

4. For discussion of rib regeneration under certain conditions, including the role of the periosteum in bone regrowth, see medical literature on rib regeneration and thoracic surgical practice.

Chapter 13

1. Dan B. Allender, writings on caregiving, healing, and the necessity of pursuing one's own freedom in order to guide others well.

About the Author

Melody Lovvorn is a writer, speaker, trauma-informed relationship and leadership coach, and pastoral care guide with nearly two decades of experience walking with women, couples, and families through crisis, healing, and restoration.

Her work is rooted in a deep passion for identity, soul care, spiritual formation, and the gentle work of returning women to the truth of who they are in God. *Grit & Grace* was born from years of accompanying women through pain, resilience, and renewal.

Melody is also the founder and Executive Director of The Togetherness Project, a 501(c)(3) nonprofit organization that invites women into healing, spiritual formation, and wholeness through online and in-person resources, teaching, mentoring, and counseling.

She is currently pursuing a Master of Theological Studies at Beeson Divinity School, further deepening the theological foundation beneath her work in soul care, spiritual formation, and restoration.

Continuing the Journey . . .

Grit & Grace was written to gently walk with weary women toward healing, wholeness, and a deeper remembering of who they are in God.

If you would like to keep going, the *Grit & Grace* Companion Bible Study Guide was created as a next step. Inside, you 'll find Scripture, reflection questions, journaling prompts, and guided space to prayerfully process your story with grace.

For the men who are reading—whether as husbands, fathers, pastors, counselors, or friends—*An Invitation to Men* offers a gentle way to better understand and honor the healing journey of a woman's heart.

If this book met you in a tender place, I'd love to stay connected.

Go to **mclodylovvorn.com/gritandgrace** for the companion Bible Study Guide, *An Invitation to Men*, next steps, resources, coaching, and ways to reach out.